EXPERIMENTS WITH MEDITATION:

AN INTEGRATED WESTERN AND EASTERN APPROACH

By

Dr. Jagtar Singh Grewal, Brig (Retd)

Become
Shakespeare
.com

First published in 2016 by

Becomeshakespeare.com
Wordit Content Design & Editing Services Pvt Ltd
Newbridge Business Centre, C38/39,
ParineeCrescenzo Building, G Block,
BandraKurla Complex, Bandra East,
Mumbai 400 051, India
T: 91 22 33040620

©
ISBN: 978-93-52017-31-7

This book is dedicated to my spiritual Guru and Guide who has bestowed His blessings on our family. Without Him we are nothing not even equal to an ant.

It is also dedicated to all those who wish to meditate and achieve final objectives of life.

Acknowledgements

First of all I must express gratitude to Almighty who has given me the strength and permission to express my views on such a subject. I am in debt to all the Ten incarnations of God in the form of Sikh Gurus. Next I am thankful to my Guru and guide who has guided me through out my life and encouraged me to narrate both direct and indirect experiences.

I am thankful to Jaspreet Kaur Grewal, our daughter in law, who suggested this topic as well as helped me to edit this book. I am also grateful to Kiran Grewal, my wife and the rest of family, which gave the required support and ideas, based on their experiences.

I am also thankful all realized souls with whom I had a chance to interact.

Dr. Jagtar Singh Grewal, Brig
(Retired)

Hockessin, DE, USA   Author

LIST OF CONTENTS

1 **Introduction** General   1

2 **Part One**   Meditation as generally understood   4

3 **Chapter One**   Definition of meditation   5

4 **Chapter Two**   Meditation as understood by followers of
                     different religions   9

5 **Part Two**   Experiences Direct and Indirect   40

6 **Chapter Three** What is meditation   41

7 **Chapter Four** Love and Faith   59

8 **Chapter Five** Purity of Mind   74

9 **Chapter Six**   Development of Virtues and weeding
                     out of Vices   85

10 **Chapter Seven** Importance of Forty Days and Years   105

11 **Chapter Eight** Achievements   108

12 **Chapter Nine** Summary   123

13   Conclusion   126

14   About the Author   127

ENGLISH TRANSLATION OF SOME OF THE TERMS USED IN THE BOOK

Serial	Hindi	English
1	Amrit vela	Time Three hours before sunrise till the sunrises
2	Astpadi	A composition which has eight stanzas
3	Bani	A composition which forms part of SGGS
4	Bhajans	Songs composed in praise of God
5	Bhakti	Combination of worship, meditation and love
6	Chalisa	A meditation program for forty days
7	Darshan	Visions of the Lord
8	Dasam Duar	Tenth opening which in the upper portion of the skull
9	Dhyana	Concentration
10	Kalas	A measure of power of God. Shri Ram incarnation was with 14 alas, Sri Krishna was with 16 Kalas. Guru NanakdevJi was with Anant Kalan (Infinite)
11	Kalyug	Age of [the demon] Kali", or "age of vice") is the last of the four stages the world goes through as part of the cycle of yugas described in the Sanskrit scriptures, within the present Mahayuga. The other ages are called Satya Yuga, Treta Yuga, and Dvapara Yuga.
12	Karma	Deeds good and bad
13	kawali	Muslim compositions in praise of Lord
14	Kirtan	Singing of Guru bani; singing praises of Lord
15	Mantra	A word or sound or a stanza repeated to aid concentration while meditating.

16	Mokh, Mukti	Salvation
17	Nishkam	Without demands
18	Pir	Muslim Saint
19	Rishi, Munni,sadhu	Saints
20	Sabad	A stanza from SGGS
21	Samadhi	A state during meditation when concentration is full, one is not aware of one's surroundings
22	Sangat	Congregation of devotees in Gurudwara Sahib
23	Satyug	See Kalyug
24	Shakti	Powers which one gains from meditation
25	Simran, Naam	Chanting of a word or stanza in praise of God
26	Yogi	One who practices Yoga

INTRODUCTION

(The greatest enemy of knowledge is NOT ignorance. It is the illusion of knowledge)

Meditation is a word commonly used but not fully comprehended by most. This word is used not only for religious purposes, but also for solving problems and focusing on issues. Quest for God or achieving salvation is perhaps as old as the humanity itself. All societies ancient, instinct or those existing at the moment have focused on this issue. Mediation as a means has been used by all of them in some form or the other. In India, Rishis, yogis, sadhus and Saints have spent many lives for this quest. Some have succeeded others have not. Buddhist monks, Muslim *Pirs* and Christian saints also have lust for God. Normal human beings who are busy in day-to-day chorus also long for God. Everyone has one's own concept of life and the way to achieve their goals, which they have set for themselves. Some believe in God others do not but all have to concentrate and make decisions, which affect their life. There are some who believe that we have only one life while others feel that there is rebirth, which is based on deeds. These kinds of debates are never ending. Sikhism has an advantage because of impact of Islam on the Indian society. Thus it has taken a leaf out of both the societies. Irrespective of whichever religion or society to which one belongs there are some basic truths of humanity, which cannot be ignored.

Questions, which flog one's mind, are many like what is meditation? How it helps to achieve goals? Is it very difficult?

Can everyone meditate? Do we have to give up our family and go to remote areas for meditation? Is it valid only for those who are followers of Indian religions? Is it all right to ask for alms? Is being wealthy an impediment to meditation? Is meditation to be done only during old age or during all stages of life? Are those who do not marry, in a better position to meditate? Does one have to become a monk to meditate? These are some of the questions, which this book attempts to answer.

Though primarily meditation is associated with spirituality, it has many applications in all chores of life. Discussion on this topic cannot be done in isolation, as it is only one of the means to achieve goals in life. Preparing the mind and body for achieving objectives, absorbing its effects and reaping the results of meditation and deeds have to be integrated. Many obstacles impede the route to final goal. These sometimes include various tests, which have to be cleared to reach the next stage. Climbing stairs is difficult but downfall can be rapid. The whole game is akin to the game of snakes and ladders where with luck one can avoid snakes. In the game it depends purely on luck but while following the spiritual path a lot depends on faith, mind control and own efforts.

Different religions suggest different paths, which confuses a person. The book brings out that all paths lead to a common objective but warns against changing paths and mixing approaches because that can lead to a confused mind, which is not conducive to do meditation. The book is laid out in two parts as under: -

Part One.   This part brings out what is commonly understood by the word meditation. It gives a general view as well as its connotation in most religions.

Part two. This part is mainly experiences. Some are direct while most are what has been gathered over a period of time by interacting with various realized souls. It covers practical ways of meditation by beginners as well as those who are in advanced stages. It also covers preparation of body and mind for meditation bringing out what to expect. However, aspects, which are normally understood like Yoga and meditation to cure diseases or other non- spiritual objectives, do not form part of the book. Cure of diseases and other miseries by spiritual means has been explained. The link between meditation, love and bhakti has been explained.

Experiments include what we experience, what we see and also learn from others experience. Practical experience of the realized souls with whom one interacts forms part of the experiments.

Exact wordings from any Gospel scripture have not been quoted in the book. The reason is that if a quote exists then proper respect has to be given to the book by keeping it at a holy place. It would imply that lesser people would read it. In the present form it is just like any other book, which can be accessed at ease. Names of Saints and realized persons have also been avoided because it can invite criticism from some which is not desirable as it can be counter productive.

On the whole the book puts across amateur experiences without using technical or spiritual jargon and suggests simple methods to follow for achieving ultimate goals in life.

Author

PART ONE

MEDITATION AS
GENERALLY UNDERSTOOD

CHAPTER ONE

DEFINITION OF MEDITATION

ﾟ◦⌒◦ﾟ

Before we proceed further, it is pertinent to examine what the general understanding of meditation is. As per Wikipedia Meditation has following connotations.

Meditation is a practice where an individual trains the mind or induces a mode of consciousness, either to realize some benefit or for the mind to simply acknowledge its content without identifying with that contender as an end by itself. The term *meditation* refers to a broad variety of practices that includes techniques designed to promote relaxation, build internal energy or life force (*qi, ki, prana*, etc.) and develop compassion, love, patience, generosity, and forgiveness. A particularly ambitious form of meditation aims at effortlessly sustained single-pointed concentration meant to enable its practitioner to enjoy an indestructible sense of well being while engaging in any life activity.

The word *meditation* carries different meanings in different contexts. Meditation has been practiced since antiquity as a component of numerous religious traditions and beliefs. Meditation often involves an internal effort to self-regulate the mind in some way. Meditation is often used to clear the mind and ease many health concerns, such as high blood pressure, depression, and anxiety. It may be done sitting, or in an active way—for instance, Buddhist monks involve awareness in their day-to-day activities as a form of mind training. Prayer beads or other ritual objects are commonly used during meditation in order to keep track of or remind the practitioner about some aspect of that training.

Meditation may involve generating an emotional state for the purpose of analyzing that state—such as anger, hatred, etc.—or cultivating a particular mental response to various phenomena, such as compassion. The term "meditation" can refer to the state itself, as well as to practices or techniques employed to cultivate the state. Meditation may also involve repeating a *mantra* with closed or open eyes. The mantra is chosen based on its suitability to the individual meditator. Meditation has a calming effect and directs awareness inward until pure awareness is achieved, described as "being awake inside without being aware of anything except awareness itself." In brief, there are dozens of specific styles of meditation practice, and many different types of activity commonly referred to as meditative practices.

Etymology

The English word *meditation* is derived from the Latin *meditatio*, from a verb *meditari*, meaning "to think, contemplate, devise, ponder".

In the Old Testament, *hāgâ* (Hebrew: הגה) means to sigh or murmur, and also, to meditate. When the Hebrew Bible was translated into Greek, *hāgâ* became the Greek *melete*. The Latin Bible then translated *hāgâ/melete* into *meditatio*. The use of the term *meditatio* as part of a formal, stepwise process of meditation goes back to the 12th-century monk Guigo II.

The Tibetan word for meditation "Gom" means "to become familiar with" and has the strong implication of training the mind to be familiar with states that are beneficial: concentration, compassion, correct understanding, patience, humility, perseverance, and so on. Emphasis on training the mind (Abhyas) is a concept peculiar to the Eastern thought.

Apart from its historical usage, the term *meditation* was introduced as a translation for Eastern spiritual practices, referred to as *dhyāna* in Buddhism and in Hinduism, which comes from the Sanskrit root *dhyai*, meaning to contemplate or meditate. The term "meditation" in English may also refer to practices from Islamic Sufism, or other traditions such as Jewish Kabbalah and Christian Hesychasm. An edited book about "meditation" published in 2003, for example, included chapter contributions by authors describing Hindu, Buddhist, Taoist, Jewish, Christian, and Islamic traditions. Scholars have noted, "The term 'meditation', since it has entered contemporary usage, is parallel to the term *contemplation* in Christianity". However, in many cases, practices similar to modern forms of meditation were simply called 'prayer'. Christian, Judaic, and Islamic forms of meditation are typically devotional, scriptural or thematic, while Asian forms of meditation are often more purely technical.

Definitions or Characterizations of Meditation: Examples from Prominent Reviews*	
Definition / Characterization	**Review**
• "[Meditation refers to a family of self-regulation practices that focus on training attention and awareness in order to bring mental processes under greater voluntary control and thereby foster general mental well-being and development and/or specific capacities such as calm, clarity, and concentration"	Walsh & Shapiro (2006)

• "*Meditation* is used to describe practices that self-regulate the body and mind, thereby affecting mental events by engaging a specific attention set.... regulation of attention is the central commonality across the many divergent methods"	Cahn & Polich (2006)
• "We define meditation... as a stylized mental technique... repetitively practiced for the purpose of attaining a subjective experience that is frequently described as very restful, silent, and of heightened alertness, often characterized as blissful"	Jevning et al. (1992)
• "The need for the meditator to retrain his attention, whether through concentration or mindfulness, is the single invariant ingredient in every meditation system"	Goleman (1988)

In India meditation is essentially a concept practiced since Vedic times. It is Lord Shiva who meditated at Amarnath followed by Parvati. Thus the way to meditate was shown by Him. From Devotees of Lord Shiva others learned the art of meditaion. During Greek invasions, this concept was studied and borrowed by them for further development. Ancient Chinese also practiced meditation as part of their spiritual attainments. From Greeks it was passed on to *Abrahamic religions*. Islamic Saints practiced meditation, which was quite similar to Indian practices. Those who understood the power of religion irrespective of which religion they followed, know very well that mediation is essential for any kind of attainment. In the next chapter let us examine how meditation forms part of each religion.

❧ ❧ ❧

CHAPTER TWO

MEDITATION AS UNDERSTOOD BY FOLLOWERS OF DIFFERENT RELIGIONS

~~~

Two Religion Theory

If we ignore rituals and minor variations, essentially there are only two prominent religions in the world today. First are those, which originated in India, called Indian religions and the second are those, which originated in the Middle East called Abrahamic Religions. Once we examine them, this grouping will become clear.

Religion is a controversial subject open to interpretation as per individual perceptions. It is a way of life where everyone establishes equilibrium with the environment. Yet there are commonalities, collective values which distinguish one society from another. Today, in the world most prominent are two religions, Christianity and Islam. Followers of rest of the religions are in minority when compared to these. The followers of both these religions have been fighting for dominance in the form of Crusades and Jihad, but the real cause has never been the religion per se but underlying greed inbuilt within human beings. Most of the comparisons are based on rituals; hence dwell on cosmetics instead of value system and terminal objectives. Indian religions on the other hand advocate passiveness and non-violence from materialistic point of view. These religions advocate quest within a person while the Western philosophy advocates search outside in the environment and materialistic based search to improve living conditions of mankind making them soft and dependent. The knowledge about Eastern religions is scanty in the Western world as they think that these religions are inferior without knowing that when India was having golden age during Gupta period, European living conditions were primitive to say the least. Owen Jones quotes Churchill in his article on "Britain's brutal colonial past" in the Tribune (2012). Churchill said to his Secretary of State for India "I hate Indians. They are beastly people with beastly religion"

In the words of Francois Gautier Â, "Like Sonia Gandhi, I am a Westerner and a brought-up catholic. My father, a very good man, was a staunch Christian; my uncle, whom I doted upon, was the vicar of the Montmartre Church, one of the most picturesque landmarks of Paris. Like Sonia Gandhi, I have lived in India for more than 40 years, and I have had the good fortune to be married to an Indian. But the comparison stops there. I did land in India with a certain amount of prejudices, clichés and false ideas, that most Westerners pick-up here and there (Tintin, Kipling, the City of Joy, Slum dog Millionaire, and so on) and I did think in the enthusiasm of my youth to become a missionary to bring back Indian ˘pagans to the true God. But the moment I stepped in India I felt that not only I had nothing much that I could give to India, but rather, that it was India which was bestowing me." **Hindus are NOT pagans**. To understand this philosophy a detailed analysis is required.

Abrahamic religions

Source. James A. Michener, in his novel 'The Source' has brought out that the source of all religions developed in the Middle East is the same. He tells the fascinating story of the Jews and other local inhabitants, of Judaism and its role in the creation of Christianity and Islam, and of the establishment of the modern state of Israel. All primordial (Prophets) who blessed our World by making appearance in the Middle East basically professed the same philosophy. On the other hand, those who appeared in India had a different approach, as we shall see later.

These religions basically believe that we have been given only one life by the God to make best use of it. After death on the day of decision that is Kayamat day or Dooms day as per one's belief, decision will be taken based on the performance on the Earth and accordingly people assigned to heaven or hell. The body, which is buried at the time of death, is thus required on the Decision day. There are other differences of course in the way of life itself, but we will restrict only to the main point to bring out the difference. These religions do not recognize prophets who appeared in India or any other place in the World. Thus the tolerance level for other faiths in their case is low. They also believe in one God and a Satan, which means there are two forces. **Satan** is a figure appearing in the texts of the Abrahamic religions who brings evil and temptation, and is known as the deceiver who leads humanity astray. Between them their faith has been adopted by all **except those** who profess Indian faith in any form may be Buddhism or Sikhism or Hinduism.

Indian religion (Eastern Thought)

"We are thankful to Indian civilization for preserving the ancient wisdom". Quote from Off Loading Stress at Work Place by **Paul Skye**, a psychologist from Australia, who advocates combination of Eastern and Western techniques to reduce stress. Indian religions believe that soul transmigrates from one birth to another taking along with it the **Karma (Deeds)** and Bhakti (a combination of meditation and worship) with the soul. The body, which is like clothes, which we wear, becomes redundant after each birth, thus burnt. The aim of each soul is reunion with The Creator being part of Him.

Karma can be: -

- **Sanchita Karma**: the accumulated result of all our actions from all our past lifetimes. This is one's total cosmic debt. Every moment of every day either one is adding to it or one is reducing it.
- **Prarabdha Karma**: the portion of our "sanchita" karma being worked on in the present life. If a person works down his agreed upon debt in this lifetime, then more past debts surface to be worked on. That is why fete keeps changing.
- **Agami Karma**: the portion of actions in the present life that add to our "sanchita" karma. If one fails to work off one's debt, then more debts are added to "sanchita" karma and are sent to future lives.
- **Kriyamana Karma**: daily, instant karma created in this life that is worked off immediately. These are debts that are created and worked off – that is. One does wrong, one gets caught and spends time in jail.

Various saints have said that the cycle of Eighty Four Lakhs or 840K (8400000) takes approximately Four Yugas to complete. The last life before human form is that of a cow. Once in Human form God gives four births as a man and three births as a women after which it all depends upon one's deeds. Thereafter, one can go back into animal life or remain in human life depending upon one's deeds and worship (Bhakti). While deeds decide next birth, Bhakti is essential for reunion with God. As per Buddhist (an off shoot of Hinduism) thought, God is energy or Force.

It is of interest to note that theory or rebirth and transmigration of soul has been validated by primary research by **Dr. Brian Weiss** in his book 'Only Love is real' and 'Same soul many bodies". He has been able to hypnotize and take his patients back up to Ninety births thereby validating most beliefs of Indian religion.

The original religion, Hinduism as we know it also believes in one God unlike general belief that it is worship of multiple gods. Bhram or Maha Vishnu is the one who has created Durga Mata in the form of Shakti (force) who in turn has three Disciples in the form of Bhrama, charged with creation, Vishnu, for administration and Shiva or Mahadev for death. Other gods (devtas) are like a Guru (teacher) who would facilitate union with God. It is of interest to note that Devtas (gods) and the devils (Rakshas) have a common father but different mother. They keep fighting with each other. Then where is the question of treating them as God of whom soul is a part? Buddhism and Jainism are offshoots of the main religion. Buddhism has a distinct advantage that it can be spread and people of other faiths can change over while this facility was not available in Hinduism, as one has to born to be a Hindu due to caste system.

The way of life advocated is so powerful that Islam and Christianity could not influence it even though rest of the world could not resist their influence. On the other hand Buddhism spread in the East with ease without any coercion and maintaining its identity with India to some extent. In India the Brahmin clergy ensured that it is contained.

Sikhism

Sikhism is the pinnacle of Indian religion amalgamating all the virtues of Indian and Middle East religions while discarding mal practices which had set in with the passage of time. Sikh means a learner. Stability was provided by Deh Dhari(God in Human Form, primordial) Gurus for 239 Years. This is the only religion where the Gurus themselves have compiled the Holy book in the form of Sri Guru Granth Sahib (SGGS). In other religions the sayings of the prophet have been compiled after the prophet had left for heavenly abode.

Continuity has been provided by Guru Bani (Recitation by Gurus) through Sri Guru Granth Sahib now for three hundred years. Such a system is unique. We will discuss some other time, the values and ethics, which make Sikhism supreme. Due to restrictions of cutting hair, some persons feel it is a difficult religion to follow but in reality it is the easiest way to salvation. It is the only religion to advocate remaining Grehast (means continue to do worldly duties and have a family) and yet attain salvation. Thus it is truly **utilitarian** religion in letter and spirit. Indian religions believe in only one God. There is NO Satan as an contemporary of God.

Differences in Both Thought processes

Abrahamic religions	Indian Religions
There is only one life	Many lives
Souls are made by GOD	Souls are part of God, thus reunion is the aim
Animals do not have souls	840K forms of life have souls, includes Nishachar (Bodiless) like ghost and so on
Body is required on Doom's day	Body is outer cover and disposable like clothes.
Heaven or hell concept	All heaven and hell is here Karma decides next birth
Please God to be comfortable here and then later in heaven	Longing for God for reunion thus second stage of love where loved is more important than self
Do good deeds. Meditation concept is vague	Bhakti is a must for reunion
Ghosts are due to accidental death and so on	Ghosts are form of live. Part of 840K
God and Satan concept	Only ONE God. Satanic activities are due to ego and desires where one thinks that one is greater than God or ignores God

Our research frame in conclusion

After considering all aspects of different religions and interacting with realized souls, conclusions are as given below.

- **Souls.** We are part of God or the Energy form and we have longing to join back. All animals, plants, and those without body have souls.

- All major scriptures are **universal**. These are like Ten Commandments, Original Bible, Vedas, Koran-e –Sharif, and Sri Guru Granth Sahib. It means they have been given by God and are available on other planets where human type of life exists in the local language. These are not affected by time. Some think that it is mentioned in the Holy Bible that Earth is the center of the Universe, which is not true. Well Vedas talk about seven skies and seven patals (worlds below ground level). This refers to our Galaxy. It means seen from Earth's point of view, seven worlds are in first and fourth quadrant while seven are in second and third quadrant. So that way we are in the center.

- There are hundred thousands of worlds in the universe unlike some who think that these are limited to 18000 or so. Guru Nanak Dev Ji showed them to the Pirjada (son of a Pir) at Bagdad when he visited there during 15th century.

- Shivji, Brahma, Vishnu and other gods are officials to run the universe. Their scale is one per galaxy.

- All primordial are part of God. Our Earth is NOT unique in having them to reform us. In fact when one nears salvation, one sees all primordial from the beginning of the universe till now and those who would come in future till end of the universe. Power of God is unique as it can be concentrated in one particle or spread in the entire universe. As per the Eastern thought it is measured in Kalas. The intelligent beings on other planets in the universe are quite similar to us but few differences like size, shape and actions. They are not like the ones shown in movies with horrible shapes.

- *God has four forms. One is Nirguna that is energy or light. Second is Sarguna that is primordial. Third is Gyan or knowledge, which is in the form of Scriptures as these are His utterances. The fourth is Nimerta or humility. Wherever there is humility He would be present.*

- Differences in religions are to suite local conditions and the time. Every time He comes to the Earth He does something unique.

Concept of meditation in Indian religions

Jainism

As per Jainism beliefs, meditation has been a core spiritual practice, one that Jains believe people have undertaken since the teaching of the Tirthankara, Rishabha. All the twenty-four Tirthankaras practiced deep meditation and attained enlightenment. They are all shown in meditative postures in the images or idols. Mahavira practiced deep meditation for twelve years and attained enlightenment. The Acaranga Sutra dating to 500 BC addresses the meditation system of Jainism in detail. Acharya Bhadrabahu of the 4th century BC practiced deep *Mahaprana* meditation for twelve years. Kundakunda of 1st century BC, opened new dimensions of meditation in Jain tradition through his books *Samayasāra, Pravachansar* and others.

Jain meditation and spiritual practices system were referred to as a salvation-path. It has three important parts called the *Ratnatraya* "Three Jewels": right perception and faith, right knowledge and right conduct. Meditation in Jainism aims at realizing the self, attaining salvation, and taking the soul to complete freedom. It aims to reach and to remain in the pure state of soul, which is believed to be pure consciousness, beyond any attachment or aversion. The practitioner strives to be just a knower-seer (Gyata-Drashta). Jain meditation can be broadly categorized to *Dharmya Dhyana* and *Shukla Dhyana*.

There exist a number of meditation techniques such as *pindāstha-dhyāna, padāstha-dhyāna, rūpāstha-dhyāna, rūpātita-dhyāna, savīrya-dhyāna*, etc. In *padāstha dhyāna* one focuses on Mantra. A Mantra could be either a combination of core letters or words on deity or themes. There is a rich tradition of Mantras in Jainism. All followers of Jainism practice chanting of mantras, irrespective of their sect, (Digambara or Svetambara). Mantra chanting is an important part of daily lives of Jain monks and followers. Mantra chanting can be done either loudly or silently in mind. Yogasana and *Pranayama* has been an important practice undertaken since ages. Pranayama – breathing exercises – are performed to strengthen the five *Pranas* or vital energy. Yogasana and *Pranayama* balance the functioning of neuro-endocrine system of body and helps in achieving good physical, mental and emotional health.

Contemplation is a very old and important meditation technique. The practitioner meditates deeply on subtle facts. In *agnya vichāya*, one contemplates on seven facts – life and non-life, the inflow, bondage, stoppage and removal of *karmas*, and the final accomplishment of liberation. In *apaya vichāya*, one contemplates on the incorrect insights one indulges, which eventually develops right insight. In *vipaka vichāya*, one reflects on the eight causes or basic types of *karma*. In *sansathan vichāya*, one thinks about the vastness of the universe and the loneliness of the soul.

Acharya Mahapragya formulated Preksha meditation in the 1970s and presented a well-organized system of meditation.

Asana and *Pranayama*, meditation, contemplation, mantra and therapy are its integral parts. Numerous Preksha meditation centers came into existence around the world and numerous meditations camps are being organized to impart training in it.

Buddhism

Buddhist meditation refers to the meditative practices associated with the religion and philosophy of Buddhism. Core meditation techniques have been preserved in ancient Buddhist texts and have proliferated and diversified through teacher-student transmissions. Buddhists pursue meditation as part of the path toward enlightenment and nirvana. The closest words for meditation in the classical languages of Buddhism are *bhāvanā*, *jhāna/dhyāna*, and *vipassana*. According to Manmatha Nath Dutt, there is hardly any difference between mainstream Hinduism's Dhyana, Dharana and Samadhi with the Buddhist Dhyana, Bhavana, Samadhi, especially as both require following the precepts (nayas and niyamas).

Buddhist meditation techniques have become increasingly popular in the wider world, with many non-Buddhists taking them up for a variety of reasons. There is considerable homogeneity across meditative practices – such as breath meditation and various recollections (*anussati*) – that are used across Buddhist schools, as well as significant diversity. In the Theravāda tradition alone, there are over fifty methods for developing mindfulness and forty for developing concentration, while in the Tibetan tradition there are thousands of visualization meditations. Most classical and contemporary Buddhist meditation guides are school-specific.

The Buddha is said to have identified two paramount mental qualities that arise from wholesome meditative practice:

- "serenity" or "tranquillity" (Pali: *samatha*) which steadies, composes, unifies and concentrates the mind;
- "insight" (Pali: *vipassana*) which enables one to see, explore and discern "formations" (conditioned phenomena based on the five aggregates).

Through the meditative development of serenity, one is able to release obscuring hindrances; it is with the release of the hindrances through the meditative development of insight that one gains liberating wisdom.

Hinduism

There are many schools and styles of meditation within Hinduism.

Traditional

Yoga is generally done to prepare one for meditation, and meditation is done to realize union of one's self, one's ātman (soul), with the omnipresent and non-dual Brahman. This experience is referred to as moksha by Hindus, and is similar to the concept of nirvana in Buddhism. The earliest clear references to meditation in Hindu literature are in the middle Upanishads and the Mahabharata, the latter includes *the Bhagavad Gita*. According to Gavin Flood, the earlier Brihadaranyaka Upanishad refers to meditation when it states "having become calm and concentrated, one perceives the self (*ātman*) within oneself".

Within Patañjali's Ashtanga yoga practice there are eight limbs leading to kaivalya "aloneness." These are ethical discipline (yamas), rules (niyamas), physical postures (āsanas), breath control (prāṇāyama), withdrawal from the senses (pratyāhāra), one-pointedness of mind (dhāraṇā), meditation (dhyāna), and finally samādhi, which is often described as the realization of the identity of the Self (ātman) with the omnipresent (Brahman), and is the ultimate aim of all Hindu yogis.

Modern

Meditation in Hinduism has expanded beyond Hinduism to the West. Mantra meditation, with the use of a japa mala and especially with focus on the Hare Krishna maha-mantra, is a central practice of the Gaudiya Vaishnava faith tradition and the International Society for Krishna Consciousness (ISKCON), also known as the Hare Krishna movement. Other popular New Religious Movements include the Ramakrishna Mission, Vedanta Society, Divine Light Mission, Chinmaya Mission, Osho, Transcendental Meditation, Oneness University, and Brahma Kumaris. According to Brahma Kumaris, meditation means, "be in remembrance of Supreme soul".

Sikhism

Sikhs gather in Gurdwara's and recite Shabad Kirtan, a vocal meditation

As per beliefs of Sikhism, simran (meditation) and good deeds are both necessary to achieve the devotee's Spiritual goals; without good deeds meditation is futile. When Sikhs meditate they aim to feel God's presence and immerse in the divine light.

It is only God's divine will or order that allows a devotee to desire to begin to meditate. Guru Nanakdev Ji in the Japji Sahib daily Sikh scripture explains, "*Visits to temples, penance, compassion and charity gain you but a sesame seed of credit. It is hearkening to His Name, accepting and adoring Him that obtains emancipation by bathing in the shrine of soul. All virtues are Yours, O Lord! I have none; without good deeds one can't even meditate.*" Japji Sahib (Stanza 21).

Nāam Japnā involves focusing one's attention on the names or great attributes of God. The practices of Simran and Nāam Japnā encourage quiet internal meditation but may be practiced vocally in the sangat (holy congregation). Sikhs believe that there are ten 'gates' to the body, the nine visible holes (nostrils, eyes, ears, mouth, urethra, anus) and the tenth invisible hole. The tenth invisible hole is the topmost energy level and is called the tenth gate or Dasam Duaar. When one reaches this stage through continuous practice meditation becomes a habit that continues whilst walking, talking, eating, awake and even sleeping. There is a distinct taste or flavor when a meditator reaches this lofty stage of meditation, and experiences absolute peace and tranquility inside and outside the body.

Followers of the Sikh religion also believe that love comes through meditation on the lord's name since meditation only conjures up positive emotions in a person, which are portrayed through our actions. The first Guru of the Sikhs, Guru Nanak Dev Ji preached the equality of all humankind and stressed the importance of living a householder's life instead of wandering around jungles meditating, the latter of which being a popular practice at that time. The Guru preached that we could obtain liberation from life and death by living a totally normal family life and by spreading love amongst every human being regardless of religion.

In the Sikh religion, kirtan, otherwise known as singing the hymns of God is seen as one of the most beneficial ways of aiding meditation, and it too in some ways is believed to be a meditation of one kind.

East-Asian religions

Taoism

"Gathering the Light", Taoist meditation from *The Secret of the Golden Flower*

Taoist or Daoist meditation has a long history, and has developed various techniques including concentration, visualization, *qi* cultivation, contemplation, and mindfulness meditations. Traditional Daoist meditative practices were influenced by Chinese Buddhism beginning around the 5th century, and later had influence upon Traditional Chinese medicine and the Chinese martial arts.

Livia Kohn distinguishes three basic types of Daoist meditation: "concentrative", "insight", and "visualization". *Ding* 定 (literally means "decide; settle; stabilize") refers to "deep concentration", "intent contemplation", or "perfect absorption." *Guan* 觀 (lit. "watch; observe; view") meditation seeks to merge and attain unity with the Dao. Based upon the *Tiantai* Buddhist practice of *Vipassanā* "insight" or "wisdom" meditation, it was developed by Daoist masters of Tang Dynasty (618–907). *Cun*

存 (lit. "Exist; be present; survive") has a sense of "to cause to exist; to make present" in the meditation techniques popularized by the Daoist Shangqing and Lingbao Schools. A meditator visualizes or actualizes solar and lunar essences, lights, and deities within his/her body, which supposedly results in health and longevity, even *xian* 仙/仚/僊, "immortality".

The (late 4th century) *Guanzi* essay *Neiye* 內業 "Inward training" is the oldest received writing on the subject of *qi* cultivation and breath-control meditation techniques. For instance, "When you enlarge your mind and let go of it, when you relax your vital breath and expand it, when your body is calm and unmoving: And you can maintain the One and discard the myriad disturbances. ... This is called "revolving the vital breath": Your thoughts and deeds seem heavenly."

The (c. 3rd century BCE) Daoist *Zhuangzi* records *zuowang* or "sitting forgetting" meditation. Confucius asked his disciple Yan Hui to explain what "sit and forget" means: "I slough off my limbs and trunk, dim my intelligence, depart from my form, leave knowledge behind, and become identical with the Transformational Thoroughfare."

Daoist meditation practices are central to Chinese martial arts (and some Japanese martial arts), especially the *qi*-related *neijia* "internal martial arts". Some well-known examples are *daoyin* "guiding and pulling", *qigong* "life-energy exercises", *neigong* "internal exercises", *neidan* "internal alchemy", and *taijiquan* "great ultimate boxing", which is thought of as moving meditation. One common explanation contrasts "movement in stillness" referring to energetic visualization of *qi* circulation in *qigong* and *zuochan* "seated meditation", versus "stillness in movement" referring to a state of meditative calm in *taijiquan* forms.

Iranian religions

Bahá'í Faith

In the teachings of the Bahá'í Faith, meditation along with prayer are both primary tools for spiritual development and mainly refer to one's reflection on the words of God. While prayer and meditation are linked, where meditation happens generally in a prayerful attitude, prayer is seen specifically as turning toward God, and meditation is seen as a communion with one's self where one focuses on the divine.

The Bahá'í teachings note that the purpose of meditation is to strengthen one's understanding of the words of God, and to make one's soul more susceptible to their potentially transformative power, more receptive to the need for both prayer and meditation to bring about and maintain a spiritual communion with God.

Bahá'u'lláh, the founder of the religion, never specified any particular form of meditation, and thus each person is free to choose his or her own form. However, he specifically did state that Bahá'ís should read a passage of the Bahá'í writings twice a day, once in the morning, and once in the evening, and meditate on it. He also encouraged people to reflect on one's actions and worth at the end of each day. During the Nineteen Day Fast, a period of the year during which Bahá'ís adhere to a sunrise-to-sunset fast, they meditate and pray to reinvigorate their spiritual forces.

Abrahamic religions

Judaism

There is evidence that Judaism has had meditative practices that go back to thousands of years. For instance, in the Torah, the patriarch Isaac is described as going *"חושׂל"* (*lasuach*) in the field—a term understood by all commentators as some type of meditative practice (Genesis 24:63).

Similarly, there are indications throughout the Tanach (the Hebrew Bible) that the prophets used meditation. In the Old Testament, there are two Hebrew words for meditation: hāgâ (Hebrew: הגה), which means to sigh or murmur, but also to meditate, and sîhâ (Hebrew: שׂיחה), which means to muse, or rehearse in one's mind.

Some meditative traditions have been encouraged in the school of Judaism known as Kabbalah, and some Jews have described Kabbalah as an inherently meditative field of study. Aryeh Kaplan has argued that, for the Kabbalist, the ultimate purpose of meditative practice is to understand and cleave to the Divine. Classic methods include the mental visualization of the supernal realms the soul navigates through to achieve certain ends. One of the best-known types of meditation in early Jewish mysticism was the work of the Merkabah, from the root /R-K-B/ meaning "chariot" (of God).

Meditation has been of interest to a wide variety of modern Jews. In modern Jewish practice, one of the best known meditative practices is called *"hitbodedut"* (תודדובתה, alternatively transliterated as "hisbodedus"), and is explained in

Kabbalistic, Hasidic, and Mussar writings, especially the Hasidic method of Rabbi Nachman of Breslav. The word derives from the Hebrew word "boded" (בודד), meaning the state of being alone. Another Hasidic system is the Habad method of "hisbonenus", related to the Sephirah of "Binah", Hebrew for understanding. This practice is the analytical reflective processes of making oneself understand a mystical concept well, that follows and internalizes its study in Hasidic writings.

The Musar Movement, founded by Rabbi Israel Salanter in the middle of the nineteenth-century, emphasized meditative practices of introspection and visualization that could help to improve moral character.

Christianity

A strong believer in Christian meditation, Saint Pio of Pietrelcina stated: "Through the study of books one seeks God; by meditation one finds him."

Christian meditation is a term for a form of prayer in which a structured attempt is made to get in touch with and deliberately reflect upon the revelations of God. The word meditation comes from the Latin word *meditari*, which means to concentrate. Christian meditation is the process of deliberately focusing on specific thoughts (e.g. a biblical scene involving Jesus and the Virgin Mary) and reflecting on their meaning in the context of the love of God.

Christian meditation contrasts with Eastern forms of meditation as radically as the portrayal of God the Father in the Bible contrasts with depictions of Krishna or Brahman in

Indian teachings. Unlike Eastern meditations, most styles of Christian meditations do not rely on the repeated use of mantras, and yet are also intended to stimulate thought and deepen meaning. Christian meditation aims to heighten the personal relationship based on the love of God that marks Christian communion.

In *Aspects of Christian meditation*, the Catholic Church warned of potential incompatibilities in mixing Christian and Eastern styles of meditation. In 2003, in *A Christian reflection on the New Age* the Vatican announced that the "Church avoids any concept that is close to those of the New Age".

Christian meditation is sometimes taken to mean the middle level in a broad three stage characterization of prayer: it then involves more reflection than first level vocal prayer, but is more structured than the multiple layers of contemplation in Christianity.

Islam

Remembrance of God in Islam, which is known by the concept *Dhikr* is interpreted in different meditative techniques in Sufism or Islamic mysticism. This became one of the essential elements of Sufism as it was systematized traditionally. It is juxtaposed with *fikr* (thinking), which leads to knowledge. By the 12th century, the practice of Sufism included specific meditative techniques, and its followers practiced breathing controls and the repetition of holy words.

Numerous Sufi traditions place emphasis upon a meditative procedure which comes from the cognitive aspect to one of the two principal approaches to be found in the Buddhist traditions: that of the concentration technique, involving high-intensity and sharply focused introspection. In the Oveyssi-Shahmaghsoudi Sufi order, for example, this is particularly evident, where muraqaba takes the form of tamarkoz, the latter being a Persian term that means *concentration*. Meditative quiescence is said to have a quality of healing, and—in contemporary terminology—enhancing *creativity*.

Tafakkur or *tadabbur* in Sufism literally means *reflection upon the universe*: this is considered to permit access to a form of cognitive and emotional development that can emanate only from the higher level, i.e. from God. The sensation of receiving divine inspiration awakens and liberates both heart and intellect, permitting such inner growth that the apparently mundane actually takes on the quality of the infinite. Muslim teachings embrace life as a test of one's submission to God.

Meditation in the Sufi traditions is largely based on a spectrum of mystical exercises, varying from one lineage to another. Such techniques, particularly the more audacious, can be, and often have been down the ages, a source of controversy among scholars. One broad group of *ulema*, followers of the great Al-Ghazali, for example, have in general been open to such techniques and forms of devotion.

In the recent years, Silsila Naqshbandia Mujaddadia under Nazim Al-Haqqani and Silsila Azeemia under Khwaja Shamsuddin Azeemi have popularized meditation or Muraqaba in various parts of the world.

Modern spirituality

New Age

New Age meditations are often influenced by Eastern philosophy, mysticism, Yoga, Hinduism and Buddhism, yet may contain some degree of Western influence. In the West, meditation found its mainstream roots through the social revolution of the 1960s and 1970s, when many of the youth of the day rebelled against traditional belief systems as a reaction against what some perceived as the failure of Christianity to provide spiritual and ethical guidance. New Age meditation as practiced by the early hippies is regarded for its techniques of blanking out the mind and releasing oneself from conscious thinking, which is often aided by repetitive chanting of a mantra, or focusing on an object. New Age meditation evolved into a range of purposes and practices, from serenity and balance to access to other realms of consciousness to the concentration of energy in-group meditation to the supreme goal of *samadhi*, as in the ancient yogic practice of meditation.

Pagan and occult religions

Religions and religious movements which use magic, such as Wicca, Thelema, Neopaganism, occultism etc., often require their adherents to meditate as a preliminary to the magical work. This is because magic is often thought to require a particular state of mind in order to make contact with spirits, or because one has to visualize one's goal or otherwise keep intent focused for a long period during the ritual in order to see the desired outcome. Meditation practice in these religions usually revolves around visualization, absorbing energy from the universe or higher self, directing one's internal energy, and inducing various trance states. Meditation and magic practice often overlap in these religions as meditation is often seen as merely a stepping-stone to supernatural power, and the meditation sessions may be peppered with various chants and spells.

Dissemination in the west

Methods of meditation have been cross-culturally disseminated at various times throughout history, such as Buddhism going to East Asia, and Sufi practices going to many Islamic societies. Of special relevance to the modern world is the dissemination of meditative practices since the late 19th century, accompanying increased travel and communication among cultures worldwide. Most prominent has been the transmission of numerous Asian-derived practices to the West. In addition, interest in some Western-based meditative practices has also been revived, and these have been disseminated to a limited extent to Asian countries. Also evident is some extent of influence over Enlightenment thinking through Diderot's Encyclopédie; although he states, "I find that a meditation practitioner is often quite useless and that a contemplation practitioner is always insane".

Ideas about Eastern meditation had begun "seeping into American popular culture even before the American Revolution through the various sects of European occult Christianity," and such ideas "came pouring in [to America] during the era of the transcendentalists, especially between the 1840s and the 1880s." But The World Parliament of Religions, held in Chicago in 1893, was the landmark event that increased Western awareness of meditation. This was the first time that Western audiences on American soil received Asian spiritual teachings from Asians themselves. Thereafter, Swami Vivekananda... [founded] various Vedanta ashrams... Anagarika Dharmapala lectured at Harvard on Theravada Buddhist meditation in 1904; Abdul Baha ... [toured] the US teaching the principles of Bahai, and Soyen Shaku toured in 1907 teaching Zen...

In the late 19th century, Theosophists adopted the word "meditation" to refer to various spiritual practices drawn from Hinduism, Buddhism and other Indian religions. Thus the English word "meditation" does not exclusively translate to any single term or concept, and can be used to translate words such as the Sanskrit *dhāraṇā*, *dhyāna*, *samādhi* and *bhāvanā*.

More recently, in the 1960s, another surge in Western interest in meditative practices began. Observers have suggested many types of explanations for this interest in Eastern meditation and revived Western contemplation. Thomas Keating, a founder of Contemplative Outreach, wrote, "The rush to the East is a symptom of what is lacking in the West. There is a deep spiritual hunger that is not being satisfied in the West." Daniel Goleman, a scholar of meditation, suggested that the shift in interest from "established religions" to meditative practices "is caused by the scarcity of the personal experience of these [meditation-derived] transcendental states – the living spirit at the common core of all religions."

Another suggested contributing factor is the rise of communist political power in Asia, which, "set the stage for an influx of Asian spiritual teachers to the West," oftentimes as refugees.

Western typologies

Ornstein noted, "Most techniques of meditation do not exist as solitary practices but are only artificially separable from an entire system of practice and belief." This means that, for instance, while monks engage in meditation as a part of their everyday lives, they also engage the codified rules and live together in monasteries in specific cultural settings that go along with their meditative practices. These meditative practices sometimes have similarities (often noticed by Westerners), for instance concentration on the breath is practiced in Zen, Tibetan and Theravadas contexts, and these similarities or "typologies" are noted here.

Progress on the "intractable" problem of defining meditation was attempted by a recent study of views common to seven experts trained in diverse but empirically highly studied (clinical or Eastern-derived) forms of meditation. The study identified "three main criteria... as essential to any meditation practice: the use of a defined technique, logic relaxation, and a self-induced state/mode. Other criteria deemed important [but not essential] involve a state of psychophysical relaxation, the use of a self-focus skill or anchor, the presence of a state of suspension of logical thought processes, a religious/spiritual/philosophical context, or a state of mental silence." However, the study cautioned, "It is plausible that meditation is best thought of as a natural category of techniques best captured by 'family resemblances'... or by the related 'prototype' model of concepts."

In modern psychological research, meditation has been defined and characterized in a variety of ways; many of these emphasize the role of attention.

In the West, meditation is sometimes thought of in two broad categories: concentrative meditation and mindfulness meditation. These two categories are discussed in the following two paragraphs, with concentrative meditation being used interchangeably with focused attention and mindfulness meditation being used interchangeably with open monitoring, Direction of mental attention... A practitioner can focus intensively on one particular object (so-called *concentrative meditation*), on all mental events that enter the field of awareness (so-called *mindfulness meditation*), or both specific focal points and the field of awareness.

One style, Focused Attention (FA) meditation, entails the voluntary focusing of attention on a chosen object. The other style, Open Monitoring (OM) meditation, involves non-reactive monitoring of the content of experience from moment to moment.

Other typologies have also been proposed, and some techniques shift among major categories.

Evidence from neuroimaging studies suggests that the categories of meditation, defined by how they direct attention, appear to generate different brainwave patterns. Evidence also suggests that using different focus objects during meditation may generate different brainwave patterns.

Effects of meditation in the classroom

Studies related to meditation in education were evaluated by to determine how it affects middle school, high school, and college students regarding academic achievement and well-being. Also compared the effectiveness of different forms of meditative programs on student outcomes. Research indicates that meditation programs have significant effects on well-being and social competence. To further explore questions related to the effectiveness of meditation in education, a sample of studies were evaluated to examine how graduation rates, academic achievement, stress reduction, and cognitive enhancement were influenced by meditation.

Transcendental meditation (TM), a form of meditation that focuses on stress reduction, was implemented to study its' impact on graduation rates, college acceptance, and dropout rates in a study on high school seniors. Volunteers practiced twice a day for 15 minutes and were taught by certified TM teachers who gave introductory hour-long lessons. Students who did not volunteer for the training were the control group, and the dependent variable was graduation. Most notably, in a comparison of 78 meditating students with high grade point average (GPA) and 78 non-meditating students with low GPA, graduation of meditating students was 82.1% compared to 66.7% for non- meditating students. This suggests that TM can positively influence the academic achievement of students.

In a similar study involving TM, identified 189 racial and ethnic minority middle school students who performed below the proficiency level on the California Standards Test (CST) in math and English at baseline. One hundred and twenty five students participated in a three-month TM program twice a day, while 64 acted as the control group and received no meditation training. For those that participated in TM, 40.7% achieved an increase of at least one level on CTS in math compared to on 15% of the control group. There was a difference in the English sections as well with 36.8% increasing a level versus $17.2% of the control group. This suggests that students who practice TM are more likely to increase test scores than those who do not.

To evaluate how meditation affects university students' cognitive abilities incorporated meditation training in a sociology class. Students were encouraged to practice at least five to ten minutes a day and asked to record their activity in a journal. They were given pretests in two executive function measures. Although no statistical significance was found, the data did show that higher reported meditation practice was associated with a more significant change in executive function abilities when pre and post-test were compared. This study highlights that there are research limitations and that more research is necessary to provide a better understanding about how meditation impacts cognitive functions.

Stress is often associated with lower academic achievement and overall well-being of students. Importantly, a study of ethnic minority high school students with exposure to high levels of violence and pressure to acculturate finds that TM is an effective way to reduce psychological distress and anxiety. The study focused on 106 students from four public high schools throughout the US and was composed of 87% minority students. Students were given pre/post test to measure psychological distress, stress, and mental health, Researchers adjusted the 7-Step TM program to cut the time spent meditating to 10–15 minutes instead of the prescribed 20 minutes recommended for adults. In reviewing the available research, there appears to be a need to explore the design of developmentally appropriate meditation practice programs for children and young adults. As suggested by, additional research may lead to a proven form of meditation that works best on young minds who are learning and would benefit from it's stress reducing benefits, point to a lack of available research as a major hurdle to evaluating studies effectively. Nonetheless, research does suggest many positive academic and personal/social benefits to those who practice medication. That, combined with its' relative ease of use make a strong argument to incorporate meditation into the school curriculum.

Secular applications

New studies say meditation is psychologically beneficial. Meditation may be for a religious purpose, but even before being brought to the West it was used in secular contexts. Beginning with the Theosophists, meditation has been employed in the West by a number of religious and spiritual movements, such as Yoga, New Age and the New Thought movement.

Meditation techniques have also been used by Western theories of counseling and psychotherapy. Relaxation training works toward achieving mental and muscle relaxation to reduce daily stresses. Jacobson is credited with developing the initial progressive relaxation procedure. These techniques are used in conjunction with other behavioral techniques. Originally used with systematic desensitization, relaxation techniques are now used with other clinical problems. Meditation, hypnosis and biofeedback-induced relaxation are a few of the techniques used with relaxation training. One of the eight essential phases of EMDR (developed by Francine Shapiro), bringing adequate closure to the end of each session, also entails the use of relaxation techniques, including meditation. Multimodal therapy, a technically eclectic approach to behavioral therapy, also employs the use of meditation as a technique used in individual therapy.

From the point of view of psychology and physiology, meditation can induce an altered state of consciousness. Such altered states of consciousness may correspond to altered neuro-physiologic states.

Today, there are many different types of meditation practiced in western culture. Mindful breathing, progressive muscle relaxation, and loving kindness meditations for instance have been found to provide cognitive benefits such as relaxation and decentering. With training in meditation, depressive rumination can be decreased and overall peace of mind can flourish. Different techniques have shown to work better for different people.

As stated by the National Center for Complementary and Alternative Medicine, a U.S. government entity within the National Institutes of Health that advocates various forms of Alternative Medicine, "Meditation may be practiced for many reasons, such as to increase calmness and physical relaxation, to improve psychological balance, to cope with illness, or to enhance overall health and well-being."

Sound-based meditation

Herbert Benson of Harvard Medical School conducted a series of clinical tests on meditators from various disciplines, including the Transcendental Meditation techniques and Tibetan Buddhism. In 1975, Benson published a book titled *The Relaxation Response* where he outlined his own version of meditation for relaxation. Also in the 1970s, the American psychologist Patricia Carrington developed a similar technique called Clinically Standardized Meditation (CSM). In Norway, another sound-based method called Acem Meditation developed a psychology of meditation and has been the subject of several scientific studies.

Many researchers have used biofeedback since 1950s in an effort to enter deeper states of mind.

(https://en.wikipedia.org/wiki/Meditation)

ॐ ॐ ॐ

PART TWO

EXPERIENCES DIRECT
AND INDIRECT

CHAPTER THREE

WHAT IS MEDITATION?

Meditations essential means concentration of inner strength (Dhyan). It is a means for achieving ultimate goal of union with God. Before achieving salvation there are number of stages through which one has to pass climbing stairs and pitfalls. There are a lot of testing moments where failure means many a step backwards. Worship (Bhakti) and Power (Shakti) go side by side but absorbing power is not an easy task, as we shall see later due to various factors like ego. We would prefer the use of the word Bhakti instead of worship because worship includes rituals while Bhakti gives you freedom from these. Bhakti implies complete devotion, love of second-degree at least meditation and obedience. During Satyug when people were pious, meditation was not very easy because almost all were God loving. In the present times there are very few who wish to meditate, therefore, achievement is possible in much shorter times as well as the path is simplified.

The paths are many but objective is one. Paths depend upon the religion one follows, the Guru who is the force, which holds one's hand and the spiritual guide one chooses. Though paths are many but they are not interchangeable which means one cannot keep crisscrossing between paths. One should follow one path; have one true Guru and one true guide till final objective is achieved. Irrespective of the path is being followed; meditation in any form should be done Nishkam, which means without any demands. Meditation should be done only to thank Him and out of sheer love for Him. While hearing, singing or reciting His praises or performing service (*Seva*), one should not ask for any boons.

Bhakti traditionally is of nine types.

Bhakti is the foundation of all spiritual practice. It is both a means and an end in itself. What is the nature of Bhakti? The Narada Bhakti Sutras say: 'It is of the nature of supreme love towards God' (2nd Sutra). How does this love towards the divine manifest itself? The Srimad Bhagavatam (7.5.23), delineates the nine ways (Navadha Bhakti) in which we can lovingly connect with God:

1) Hearing about God (Shravana)
2) Chanting His Name and Glory (Kirtana)
3) Remembering Him (Smarana)
4) Serving His Lotus Feet (Pada Sevana)
5) Worshipping Him as per the Scriptures (Archana)
6) Prostrating before Him (Vandana)
7) Being His Servant (Dasya)
8) Befriending Him (Sakhya)
9) Offering Oneself to Him (Atma Nivedana)

Hearing about God means to listen to Recitation of Guru Bani (Holy Scriptures) either by singing (Kirtan) or simple recitations. It helps to concentrate when one listens with open mind in a peaceful atmosphere with mind fully engrossed in it. Listening while working or without understanding meanings does not allow concentration. Modern technology has simplified listening to a large extent where one does not have to physically go where the Lords praises are been sung or recited. Live Kirtan from various Gurudwaras and other religious places is available through Internet. Compact discs, Mobile applications and other devices are in plenty. All Gospels are very powerful but common person does not understand scriptures like Vedas, which are in Sanskrit. Gurubani on the other hand is easily understood and soothing. However, there are many people of European and African origin who have converted to Sikhism. They have limited knowledge of Punjabi but are able to follow by using English translation. In most Gurudwaras specially those which are in USA, Canada, UK, Australia and other countries display on projector what ever is being recited with meaning for all to follow. Guru Nanak Devji has devoted Four Pauries (Stanzas) of Japji Sahib to listening where it is clearly mentioned that concentration is achieved by listening. Bhajans are sung in praise of the Lord but are not Gospel. Those, which were recited by Meerabai, Surdas and others, help in concentration. To begin with, while listening eyes must either remain closed or focused on the Lotus feet of the Lord or the Deity. At later stages when the Lord resides in the heart focus changes. Followers of **Abrahamic** religions also believe in hearing and singing praises of the Lord in their places of worship for instance, Kawali is widely used by followers of Islam.

Reading from Scriptures (Path) helps but it can soon turn into a ritual unless care is exercised. While reading one should contemplate on the meanings in the mind while the tongue recites. Best is to memorize by heart few selected Banies or chapters. Even normal prayers that are recited can be very powerful. For example, when some one recites Japji Sahib one tends to recite it while bathing or otherwise while doing some work and be done with it. That actually has no effect. SGGS begins with the word Ekomkar. The expansion of this word is Japji Sahib. Expansion of Japji Sahib is the whole SGGS. When one sits down to recite or listen one should concentrate on the Lotus feet of the Guru. Soon one would be in a state of bliss (reach Sachkhand). Then in the end is the slok which brings one back to the real world. This way reciting prayers or path or scriptures is meditation. Another aspect of Japji Sahib is that Guru Nanakdev Ji has used the word NO many times but always-in positive sense. For example "There is no end of God and His creation." It implies that He is endless. While reciting or listening though the ears and eyes are tuned to what is being listened or read, the mind should be churning over the meanings as it helps to concentrate.

If one has not been able to memorize the Bani then best is to listen. Other banies, which are based on praising the Lord, are Jaap Sahib and Akal Ustati. Sikhs are required to recite Five banies in the morning, Rehras in the evening and Kirtan solah just before going to bed. In addition Sukhmani Sahib is recited any time during the day. For those who are working it is very difficult to recite all of them with the concentration described above. Therefore, for beginners it is recommended that either Japji sahib or Jap Sahib is recited with full concentration and rest of the banies with as much concentration as possible. Later in the evening Rehras should also be done with full concentration. Reciting Sukhmani Sahib with full concentration would result in tremendous gains though it is not easy for beginners. Followers of Hindu religion can structure recitation of slokas, or bani like Sri Bhagwat Geeta or Hunuman Chalisa accordingly. There are set rules given at for those who recite Hunuman Chalisa at http://

cosmoread.com/chanting-rules-regulations-hanuman-chalisa/. Tulsidasji composed hanuman Chalisa when he was sick. After reciting it he recovered from sickness. With beads of 108, it can be recited in about six to seven hours. But to gain from the recitation one must have faith and have no bad thoughts. The followers of Islam must offer five Namaz with full concentration. It would be of interest to note that when the Nawab and Kazi asked Guru Nanak Dev Ji to join them for Namaz, Guru Sahib readily agreed but did not recite it. On being asked He replied that during the recitation the mind of the Nawab was focused on selling some horses while the Kazi was thinking of the newly born calf at home. So there was no body with whom He could join for offering Namaz. Proper way to offer Salat (Namaz) is given on the website http://www.islamicacademy.org.

Reading of SGGS with breaks (sehaj path) or akhand path (without break) is a common practice, which bears results provided performed properly. During Akhand path first 97 angs(Pages) should be heard by most family members. Thereafter, at least one family member should be in attendance while others prepare meals extra for bhog and for the *pathies* (clergy men who are reciting the path). At home there should not be viewing of normal TV programs extra. At the time of closing ceremony there is a tendency of inviting whole lot of relatives and friends with meals prepared by catering services, which turns it into a ritual. Concentration should be on service of the pathies. For sehaj path unless done by oneself, one should sit down and listen when the path is being recited. Hindus have recitation of Ramayana as Akhand path, which can be done in a similar manner. Even Guru Gobind Singhji has mentioned that Ramayana is valid in all yugas (Jugo Jug atal).

Next is Simran and reciting Lords praises. What happens if some one is called by his name? He would but naturally respond. God's names are generally description of the qualities attributed to Him. So when we utter His name, He is likely to respond better than merely thinking about Him. This practice is very common from ancient times. During Satyug, The word recommended was Vasudeva, During Treta Yug it was Ram, Duapar yug sadhus concentrated on Hari while during Kalyug it is Gobind. Guru Nanakdevji combined all four into Vaheguru. Sikhs chant Mul-Mantra up to "Nanak Hosi bhi sach" also. Sikhs believe that Ekomkar is beej- mantra (seed), Mul-Mantra is first stanza of SGGS, and Mala- Mantra is Japji Sahib. Any word is good enough as long as concentration is achieved. A king during ancient times recited mara- mara (instead of Ram- Ram) and achieved salvation. For beginners time wise early hours about three hours before sunrise (Braham Mahurat or Amrit vela) is the best time to recite. A comfortable posture siting alone in a quiet place is recommended. The postures recommended for Yoga (84 Asans) may be good for health and the body but from meditation point of view are not recommended by SGGS. The word to recite can also be the one given by Guru or the Guide. Followers of Islam can recite "Rahim" or any other wording given the their guide. Christians generally recite a stanza from the Holy Bible.

In the first stage one recites with tongue leading to second stage when the tongue does not move. In the third stage with each breadth Simran continues. In the fourth stage the reciting continues in the mind and body 24 × 7. While reciting Simran concentration of mind should be on the lotus feet. Slowly the level of concentration will increase leading to "Samadhi". This is the stage when one is detached from this world and totally engrossed in the thoughts of lord. In such a state need for sleep or eating food disappears. Samadhi and sleep have a lot in common as during both, one is not aware of one's surroundings, wealth or belongings. As such the body is at rest.

While meditating, concentration also energizes the body. As per Sehaj Yoga beliefs, energy resides in two and a half coils at the end of the spinal cord. During meditation it rises and energizes the body opening the Tenth Gate that is on the skull. **DASAM DVAR** (Sanskrit Dasamadvara), literally meaning **"tenth gate"**, has been referred to in SGGS signifying the door to enlightenment and vision being only through Naam, Dhan(donations), service and Humility.

This term originated from the Hathayogic system, where it is also known as the brahmrandhra, moksadvara, mahapatha, madhya marga or even the **"Dasam Duara"**; these terms are frequently used in the esoteric literature of medieval India.

It is a term of religious physiology and its significance lies in its being a concept in the framework of soteriological ideology. The nine apertures (navdvaras) opening towards outer side of the body serve the physical mechanism of human personality but when their, normally wasted, energy is consciously channelized towards the self, the tenth gate or the dasam dvar opens inside the body and renders a hyper-physical service by taking the seeker beyond the bondage of embodied existence.

Also called holes or streams, these nine doors are the: eyes, ears, nostrils, mouth, anus, and urethra. All are vital organs of the human being. In the Buddhist caryapadas or hymns of spiritual practice, the dasama dvara is also called vairocana-dvara, the brilliant gate or the supreme gate.

It is this energy, which enables Sadhus or seekers to meditate on Himalayan Mountains. Scientist cannot gauge this energy as yet like two hundred years back no one could imagine that atom can produce so much energy. When someone is in akhand Samadhi (without a break), the body can generate so much heat that temperature can rise beyond boiling point of water. When Tansen recited Deepak raag his body was on the verge of burning. It had to be cooled down by recitation of Megh raag by his daughter. Those meditating do not require such cooling because they can control their body temperatures. When required the body temperature can drop to required levels. When energy flows through the tenth gate, a feeling of coolness can be felt on the head. While meditating do not think about what is to be done during the day. In other words this is not the time to plan one's day but to concentrate for meditation.

Serving His lotus feet and being His servant is next in importance. It essentially means service (seva). Before we understand service it is necessary to ponder over forms of God.

- First is **Nirgun Srup** which means formless. This is what is commonly understood as God, Allah, or Bhagwan or Force. It is very difficult to imagine any shape attributed to this form. From meditation point of view it is difficult to focus on to this form at least in the beginning. After certain stage one may be able to focus on light or even blankness.
- Second form refers to **Sargun Sarup**. Whenever there is a problem in the world, He appears in human form to solve

the problem. Once He appeared as Narsingh form which means half animal and half human. The human form is referred to as primordial. When ever He appears in this form He never addresses Himself as God but as son of God or His slave and so on. This form is easier to concentrate on. Later on one may experience visions also.

- Third form is **knowledge** form in the form of Gospel scriptures, which have been obtained from Him by various prophets for us. May it be Ten Commandments Holy Bible or Vedas or SGGS, they all are gospel, therefore, they are forms of God. It has been mentioned by Guru Arjan Devji in SGGS it self that it is a form of God. For followers of Sikhism, It is Guru and thus God. All the Ten forms of Guru Nanak Devji were incarnation of God as such *Sargun Sarup* mentioned here in. It is easy to concentrate on SGGS or in the presence of SGGS.

- Fourth Form is **Humility**. Wherever humility is present He is there; wherever ego resides, He leaves the place. Baba Srichandji, son of Guru Nanak Devji while talking to Guru Ramdassji disclosed that when he asked Guru Nanak Devji where to search for Him after he leaves His body, Guru Nanakdev Ji replied, that He could be found wherever humility (Nimarta) is. Guru Nanakdev Ji has referred to Himself as the lowest being at many places in SGGS. When Guru Ramdas Ji washed the lotus feet of Baba Srichand Ji and dried them with His beard, Babaji commented that he could see the same humility (Nimarta) in Guru Ramdas Ji, which His father, Guru Nanak Devji had.

Out of the type of Bhakti described in the beginning of the chapter, second and third forms are important from concentration point of view while the **fourth and seventh** are essential for service, which can be performed in three ways as under: -

1. **Service of the Guru**, which could be SGGS, or **the deity** whom one worships. As per beliefs of Sikhism, the Guru after Guru Gobind Singhji left this world with His body is SGGS, which is to be worshiped as if it is a living Guru. The service of SGGS requires lot of dedication day and night. Normally clergy preforms this service in the Gurudwaras but many people have SGGS at their homes. Space permitting, it is recommended that those Sikhs who wish to meditate should have SGGS at home. Minimum requirement is of a bed six feet by three feet with space to sit around it. Otherwise a quite corner should by identified where one can sit and meditate in peace and tranquility. In such cases to achieve results, one has to be dedicated and poise treating their own home as Gurudwara or temple where those activities, which are not approved by the Guru, are not carried out. Service of the lotus feet can be carried out first in imagination. Later when Guru desires gives one an opportunity. Only those who have experienced it can narrate. In fact all those who meditate may belong to any religion, must treat their homes as that of God given to them on rent by Him. That would imply that only those activities, which are approved by Him, are carried out in that house. There is no place for black money deeds, telling lies or making plans for cheating people, consumption of liquor and drugs in that house. In fact they should not allow people to enter their house after consuming liquor or drugs otherwise negative effects would set in. There is lot of controversy about offering food to the Guru before one eats (Bhog Lagana) especially among Sikhs who feel that treating SGGS like a deity or image is not

correct. They forget that SGGS is to be treated like a living Guru. The correct way to do it is that the food should be prepared with love and affection with full concentration of mind. Then it should be taken to the room where SGGS is. Placed on a table, which is readily accessible to SGGS and request made through prayer to SGGS to consume it and to give permission for it to be consumed by devotees. After reasonable time it is taken back and added to the food prepared for the devotees or the family as the case may be. Hindus offer it to the deity. Many people feel that it is a ritual, which it is not. One may think that the quantity of food remains the same. It does remain same because from full if one takes out full it still remains full. Sikhs may note that there are many stanzas (Sabads) in SGGS, which mention about a request to God to reside in one's heart but there is only ONE which states that a devotee resides in His heart. That sabad refers to Bhagat Namdevji when he offered milk to God. There was a lady who used to offer bhog to her Guru/Guide daily with love and affection even though the Guru/Guide had left His body long back. One day she was sick and lying on the bed. She called for someone to give her food but there was no one around as the person in attendance thought while she is sleeping he could perform some other duties. Soon she saw a person standing near her bed with a cloth covering His face holding a plate full of eatables. She took the plate and started eating thinking it is person who normally attended to her. She narrated that it was the tastiest food she had ever eaten. Then she looked towards Him and asked, "Who are you?" The person removed the cloth covering His face so that she could see her Guru/Guide standing in front of her. The Guru said, "You prepare food for me daily so I can also give you when you need." She was awed and could not speak a word after such a darshan. (Names are not mentioned on purpose because those who may not have faith may criticize which can have ill effects).

Bhagat Dhanna is famous as a true devotee who was bestowed with not only powers but also God Himself came to help him to plough his fields. Bhagat Dhanna Ji had seen the Pundit in the temple offering milk and food to the deity. On enquiring he was told that the deity accepts offerings given by the pundit. Bhagat Dhanna Ji requested the pundit to give him an idol so that he could also worship. The Pundit handed him over a stone, in lieu of the idol saying that he could worship it. Bhagat Dhanna Ji took it home and offered the idol food. He refused to eat until the idol accepted his offerings. For thirteen days the Bhagat Ji stayed in the room waiting for the idol to accept his offerings. At last God had to relent and give him darshan to consume the food he had to offer. Thereafter, He was blessed and given all the knowledge (nirmal Gyan). People started respecting the Bhagat Ji, which was detested by the pundit. The pundit challenged him stating if His idol (Thakhur) was powerful then it would swim in the river. The entire village witnessed the idol and the Bhagat Ji swimming in the river by just holding on to the idol. Such is the power of love for God. God only sees whether the devotee love Him or not. Rituals extra do not matter.

Another example is of a child who was six years old. The family is devoted, as the father is a realized soul. The mother of the child prepared burfi (a type of Indian sweats prepared from milk). She told the child to take it to the prayer room and offer it to the Saint/guide whose painting is placed along side SGGS. It is of interest to note that the saint had left His body many years ago. The child spent sometime inside the room. When he came out he said to his mother, "One thing I could not understand. How Babaji came out of the painting, took two pieces of the barfi and went back into the painting." The mother explained to him the logic of bhog and what devotion and love is all about.

Those who are not realized souls also have many such experience. Before offering the food no one tastes the food. It is only consumed after the bhog. Many times when it is offered to SGGS or the deity a voice tells a person if there is some shortcoming in any dish.

Another type of service that bears fruit is waving of **ceremonial whisk (Chor Sahib)** over SGGS or the deity one worships. While performing this service one do Simran also.

2. As we shall see later a human guide is required for meditation for the beginners. **Service of the guide** or Saint or sadhu or simply a person who is far ahead on the path of meditation is the second method. Those who look after the guide with dedication progress at a fast pace provided they obey all his commands. In present times it is not very easy to find a proper guide because many are only looking for money pretending to be pious. Later on we will examine this aspect in details but an acid test could be "those who take help of God to control people to gain monetary or other benefits should be avoided. Those who lend their shoulders to support the devotee and unite them with God are to be followed. For full definition of a true guide one should refer to Eighth and Ninth Ashtpadi of Sukhmani Sahib. Guru Amardassji set an example by bringing water from Vyas River for his Guru Angad Devji daily for 12 years when he was in his sixties and seventies. He never turned his back towards the Guru so went backwards to the river and return facing the Guru from Khadur Sahib to the river near Gobindwal. A devotee once

narrated his experience of washing the feet of his Guide who was a well-known and respected realized soul. He was given the opportunity once to perform the service. After washing he was asked to take the tub to the garden and empty it on the lawn. After going outside, first of all he took few sips of the *charanamrit* (water in the tub) and also washed his face with it. Still there was plenty of it left in the utensil. When he tried to empty it he found that not a single drop fell on the ground. When he looked up, he had vision of many sur, nar, munijan, rishis not only of our planet but also of many other worlds carving for a drop of the *charnamrit*. This happens because a realized soul who has been meditating for thousands of years during many births comes in human form rarely.

3. **Third form** of service is of devotees and humanity as such. Service in the kitchens at Gurudwara Sahib, and other religious places or at various orphanages and Ashrams forms part of this service. Serving devotees can be in the form of taking care of their footwear when they come to the holy place, or serving and preparing food or cleaning the premises or any other type of service which may be required. This service is to be preformed without ego, as we shall see later.

Other forms of worship are either part of the service or rituals, which do not have much significance. The ninth type implies surrender. It means surrender one's ego. Therefore, Bhakti implies basically singing or reciting His praises, Simran, service and total surrender. Love for God is prime consideration. Slowly when one progresses, the differences in various religions and or the primordial that have blessed the Earth disappear. At final stages, one may have vision of all the primordial not only those who belong to Earth but also those who are of the entire universe of past present and future means those who are yet to come.

Guru Nanak Devji has described five stages. First is Dharam, which means the physical stage in which we all live in this world. Here we have different names and are rated as per our deeds. During the **second stage** one gains knowledge as to how to achieve salvation Knowledge is of three types. First is *Chunj Gyan* (little or superfluous knowledge gained through reading some reviews). Second type of knowledge is *Pothi Gyan* (gained by going through scriptures). The third type of knowledge is *Nirmal Gyan* (given by God when one becomes realized soul or obtained through a realized soul). In the **third stage** one strives for final objective by practicing the knowledge gained. In the **Fourth stage**, God is pleased and showers His blessings. In the **Fifth and final** stage one achieves the goal of union with God.

"In true meditation, there is neither meditator nor meditation; there is only the meditated. In true love there is no lover or love; there is only the beloved. In true prayer there is no worshiper and worship; there is only the worshipped." A Saint

What is the best age for meditation?

SGGS says that **all three phases** of life that is childhood, youth and old age are a waste without meditation. Those who have accumulated meditation to their credit can start meditating at a very early stage in life. One should be initiated into prayers, meditation and given knowledge about one's religion by the parents. Gradually during youth it gains momentum, which can then continue during old age. Best time to do service and meditation is between thirty to sixty years of age. Unfortunately it clashes with the productive years when one can earn money. Thus a balance is required depending upon nature of work and health.

During child hood depending upon the atmosphere in the house children pick up good or bad habits. If parents are devotees, then children naturally follow. Sometimes the child has accumulated credits in meditation in the previous births but the parents are not God loving which creates cognitive dissonance in the mind of the child. Such children sometimes go astray or start following some other religion.

Handling of Crystal Children

Crystal children have been sent by God to save this world. They have been coming from time to time. They are spiritually awakened, like to be left alone and have some sort of powers out of those mentioned in the following chapters. They require special handling otherwise due to conflict between requirements of materialistic world and their inner thinking there is conflict in the mind. They are prone to have Asthma. They learn only from those whom they mentally accept as teachers hence require good schools. In later part of life if the spouse is not spiritually awakened the marriage is unlikely to succeed.

Doreen Virtue, noted author and expert on Star Children, has written about the characteristics of Crystal children. She says these characteristics may include:

- Have large, communicative eyes and an intense stare.
- Are highly affectionate.
- Begin speaking later in life, but often uses telepathy or self-invented words or sign language to communicate.
- Love music and may even sing before talking.
- Are extremely connected to animals and nature.
- Are often very interested in rocks, crystals, and stones.

- Are extremely artistic.
- Are highly empathic and sensitive.
- Are forgiving and generous to others.
- Draw people and animals near them and love attention.
- Often have good sense of balance and are fearless when exploring high places.
- Often see or hear angels and spirit guides - both their own and others'.
- Dislike high-stress environment where there are many distractions.
- Dislike loud/sharp sounds.
- They dislike bright and unnatural lights.
- Often enjoy choosing their own meals and/or time when they eat them.
- Often speak about universal love and healing.
- Sometimes show healing gifts at young ages.
- Don't react well to sugar, caffeine, or unnatural foods/chemicals.
- Dislike fighting or refuse to keep an argument going very long.
- Often show strength in telekinesis (or Psycho kinesis).
- Often amplify emotional energies they gain from their environment (such as negative energies).
- Can become uncomfortable when around electrical devices for too long (watching TV, computer, etc.), sometimes resulting in a trance-like state.
- Sometimes they seem 'clingy' to their parents until age of 4 or 5 years.
- Often stare at people for long periods of time (this allows them to read a person and find out more about them through their own personal memories and energy).
- Can sometimes be manipulative and throw tantrums if they cannot create a reality that is good for them.

- Are easily over-stimulated and need to meditate or be left alone often to replenish themselves.
- Don't usually have trouble with fear or worry.
- They enjoy discussing spiritual or philosophical topics.
- May appear to be looking at nothing or talking to no one (sign of clairvoyance and/or clairaudience).
  (http://www.starchildren.info/crystal.html)

It is important for the parents to recognize such children and bring them up in an atmosphere where they can meditate. It is best to keep them away from alcohol, tobacco and non-vegetarian products.

Sikhs and Christians have concept of baptism. Guru Gobind Singh Ji started this for the Sikhs. Generally there is lot of discussion about restrictions and gains, but the most important gain, which is generally overlooked, is that the Karma account of those who are baptized passes on to the Guru from Dharamraj. Most saints now a days do not recommend carrying of sword (Kirpan) as that is redundant in the modern context.

However, achievement is only possible if **love for God** is present and mind is pure. These aspects we shall examine in following chapters.

❧ ❧ ❧

CHAPTER FOUR

LOVE AND FAITH

Love

Love of God is the main factor, which unites all religions. Guru Gobind Singhji has clearly stated that only those whose who love God can hope to find Him. There is no other way. But love itself has four forms or one can say there are four types of love.

First is need based. It implies that there is a need for God for selfish motives. These motives could be worldly or for ultimately residing in heaven. This type of bond can exist between any two persons also. For example such a bond exists between the employer and the employee. One wants to remain happy in this world and also keep God pleased so that after death one has a place in heaven. The worldly demands are requirement of the body not of the soul because it is the body, which requires all the pleasures of life. Most people pray hard to have their demands fulfilled. Once they achieve them, they may not have time even to visit Gurudwara, temple, church or mosque depending upon faith which one follows. Meditation by many individuals including Ravana is a classical example of this kind of love.

Second type of love is selfless bonding means sacrifice. A parent loves the child not because of expectations from the child but because the parent wants to give the best to the child. Similarly, a seeker loves God because of suffering due to separation from Him. When this sort of bonding takes place worldly desires disappear giving way to longing to be with Him. In fact SGGS goes to the extent of stating that neither kingdom nor salvation is desired at this stage. Only attachment to His lotus feet is the desire. Here the belief that body is destructible while soul is part of God plays an important role. Attachment with near and dear ones gives way to the Creator alone. Pleasures of life required by the body are no longer important. For such kind of love it is not necessary to be poor or rich. Like the famous King Janak, one can have lot of wealth; yet remain detached from it like the lotus flower in the water or the duck swimming in water without wetting its feathers.

Third type of love is when one is engrossed in love 24 × 7. Scanning the literature we find two examples of such a love between humans. First is Shakuntala engrossed in thoughts of King Dashyunt when Rishi Durwasa curses her. Second is of Heer engrossed in thoughts of Ranja when she steps over the cloth spread by Kazi while he was offering Namaz to God. On being asked that why she did not see the cloth, she replied that she was engrossed in thoughts of a human but the Kazi was engrossed in the thoughts of God then how did he see her going over the cloth. In such a state while working, eating or sleeping one is engrossed in the thoughts of the Lord. Such stage comes after one is deeply immersed in meditation.

Fourth type of love refers to soul mates that return as relatives after every birth. It has been explained by Dr. Brien Weiss adequately is his books like "Soul Mates".

First type of relation with God or Guru does not last very long. During meditation also thoughts keep returning to the desires and wishes. God is also happy to grant such worldly wishes and be done with it. Such people do not realize that what ever their problems are because of their deeds during the present and past lives. They ask for a wish based on their problem, which is granted, by God but the sin due to which the problem arose stands. It would then manifest in another problem, which means cycle of asking, and granting is never ending with end result being zero. The entire meditation is wasted. Some people ask for more wealth, which may require sinful activities to maintain it or to increase it further since such people are likely to be greedy. Thus at the end of the present life they would have neutralized their positive deeds and collected negative deeds. Thus at the end balance would run into minus which can lead to the next birth in non-human forms or human life full of miseries.

To do effective meditation one requires to develop Second degree of love which is selfless, without any demands, pure longing to unite with His lotus feet. Such a state then results in a bonding where love between God and the devotee or between the Guru and the Guide is mutual. The tears, which are caused by this kind of love, are priceless.

As one meditates more, one will be able to see inner vistas. The second practice of meditation is listening to the inner sound. One concentrates to listen to the inner sound current (Anahad). Once a person is tuned in to the divine melody, he can travel on the sound current to higher realms of consciousness.

Meditation is a way to connect with divine power. One might feel permeated with a feeling of love, which engulfs and fulfills oneself. We experience a profound peace and bliss unlike any we can find in this world. The meditation process helps us at two levels. First, it relaxes us physically. Second, it puts us in a state where we are absorbed in bliss and become oblivious to problems of the outer world.

By meditating on the inner light and sound, we are placed in contact with the radiant energy coming from realms that lie beyond the physical world. There is a powerful current of divine love, consciousness and bliss. Meditation does not literally eliminate problems of life, but gives us a new perspective. We become detached from suffering because we are able to find a spiritual anchor. Through meditation not only can we learn the art of living, which helps' us overcome life's stresses and strains, but also discover a way to experience the Divine."

Faith, Trust and belief

Belief implies that the person, in whom one believes, will do what you ask the person to do. It would generally be restricted to a particular task or wish. Similarly when the love is of the First degree, one believes that God will grant one what ever has been asked for. This is the weakest type of bonding among belief, trust and faith.

Trust is a stronger bond than belief since it has stronger roots. One is sure that the work will be done. However, it does not imply complete surrender. One can waver and loose trust even if there is small misunderstanding. Beginners who want to meditate can loose trust easily if they run into difficulties or encounter problems or do not get immediate results.

Faith trust and believe stem from love and are closely linked to the stages of love. In the first stage, where love is need based it is just a belief that the other person will do what is expected. It can easily be broken if the other person gets a better deal. The Second stage results in 'Trust' which is **a positive expectation that the trustee will not—through words; actions, or decisions—act opportunistically. The two most important elements of our definition are that it implies familiarity and risk.** The term *opportunistically* refers to the inherent risk and vulnerability in any trusting relationship. Trust involves making oneself vulnerable as when, for example, we disclose intimate information or rely on another's promises. What are the key dimensions that underline the concept of trust? Recent evidence has identified five ingredients of trust: **integrity, competence, consistency, loyalty, and openness**

There are three types of trust in organizational relationships: deterrence-based, knowledge-based, **and** identification-based. Deterrence based is negative and generally in the first stage only. Knowledge based refers to predictability of behavior based on past experience. Best is identification based; but it can hurt most if broken.

Faith is the highest form of trust where one completely surrenders to a leader, or to a life partner or to God thus possible only in Second and third stages of love and devotion. Putting oneself in the hands of God is the First lesson of Sri Guru Granth Sahib given in the First Pauri (stanza) of JapJi Sahib. Without any kind of faith one would drift along the life as it comes, which may result in mental agonies or stress.

Faith implies obedience of the highest order. Having faith that whatever God is doing to shape your life is the best path for oneself, helps us to live peacefully and meditate. We do not know future nor we are aware of our past lives. Seeing what ever is happening in the present we feel a particular course is better for us. May it be identifying a life partner or work related or buying property and so on. God knows our past deeds and also our future. If we love Him then He also loves us. If that were so, then it is definite that He would chalk out the best path for us depending on our deeds. Whatever we have done in the past in the present life or the past lives results either in rewards or suffering. Justice is dispensed by Him absolutely fairly though we feel that it is not so because we do not know our deeds but expect rewards. That is why the Second Sikh Guru, Sri Guru Angad Devji says that human beings sow poison but expect nectar in return. Then he asks, "What kind of justice is this?"

In the early decades of Twentieth century, a disciple of a Saint at Bhuchokalan near Bathinda, Punjab used to bring milk for Him daily. One day while he was walking with the milk can on his head, a big thorn stuck on his foot. With great difficulty he managed to reach the place where Babaji lived. En-route he was thinking that he was performing holy service then why was he facing such a problem. When he arrived, Babaji reading his mind said, "Sul de ke Suli se bacha liya". (By giving you pain of the thorn I have saved you from being hanged which was written in your destiny). This incident demonstrates that He mellows down the sufferings, which would have otherwise been very severe if one did not love God.

When Guru Gobind Singhji was at Anandpur Sahib, many kings of hill states were apprehensive of the consequences of military power being developed by Him. One of the kings send a trusted minister to the Guru's court disguised as a devotee to get exact details of what was going on over there. When he arrived at the court of the Guru, he was totally awed and became a hard-core devotee. Due to his bhakti, he had the image of the lotus of the Guru planted in his eyes. After some time elapsed, the king sent another spy to recall the minister to submit his report. The minister came back and was asked to narrate all the military build up which he had observed. The minister who had turned a devotee started singing praises of the Guru. The king got angry and stated that since the minister has turned hostile; he should be taken to a remote place and his eyes punctured with hot metal rods. Accordingly, the soldiers took him to a remote place and punctured his eyes with red-hot iron rods. After some time when he opened his eyes, he did not feel any pain nor felt any problem with his vision. He walked straight towards Anandpur Sahib reaching there in a few days. Exactly at the time when his eyes were being pierced, blood started oozing out from the lotus feet of the Guru. Devotees quickly bandaged the feet but could not muster the courage to ask as to what had happened. When the minister reached Anandpur Sahib and did dandaut (to lie down in front of the feet of the Guru to pay respect; a sign of complete surrender) he found that the lotus feet were bandaged. On enquiring the Guru said it is all because of him and asked him as to what image he had in his eyes. Then he narrated the whole incident to all present in the court. This is what happens when one has complete faith.

A book published by the disciples of Bhai Mani Singh who wrote SGGS when Guru Gobind Singhji dictated the SGGS at Damdama Sahib, mentions about a true story. A girl used to listen to explanations given by a pundit. The pundit said that if one has faith then even a river, which may be deep, could be crossed without feeling the water to be no more than knee deep. Her house was on the other side of a river. Since she had faith she could cross the river without any problem. She used to come for the Pundit's sermons very often. In the month of September during Shrads (time when Hindus offer food to their ancestors) she asked Pundit Ji to come to her house to perform Puja and accept the offering on behalf of the ancestors. The Pundit Ji agreed and accompanied her. On reaching the river, she said let's go and started moving towards the waterline. Pundit Ji got wild and asked her as to what were her intentions. Did she want him to be drowned? Promptly the Pundit Ji went back. She continued to walk on the riverbed and called some other pundit for the puja. The moral of the story is that if one listens with faith then one can benefit even though an unrealized soul may be giving sermons.

Having faith implies **obedience of the highest order** without questioning motive or results. Obedience has many connotations. **First** is a simple desire of the beloved. For those who are completely devoted a desire by God or the Guru or the Guide is as good as an order. **Second** type is the order given by the beloved. Disobedience of such an order can have repercussions, which can be in the form of the withdrawal of His blessings and protection. **Third** type is warrant or summons (*Cheeri*) issued by the beloved. Disobedience of such a warrant would result in punishment. **Fourth** is more severe form of order, which is like the judgment passed by the court. It is called "Hikmaat". Those who have read "Zaffarnama" a letter written by Sri Guru Gobind Singhji to Aurangzeb would know that after reading the letter Aurangzeb died.

We should differentiate between fear and regard (Dhar and Bhai as stated in SGGS). Actions of a person due to fear are to avoid revenge or punishment meted out by the person whom one fears. Bhai or regard arises out of love and respect. Sri Guru Nanak Devji says that the whole universe functions due to Bhai. A person who loves God is fearless. He is not afraid of any one as long as he is in service or worship of God. He would always do correct deeds and speak the truth.

A true story about Hakuin Zenji (The Speaking tree TOI)

Hakuin Zenji, an 18th century Japanese Zen master, was known for his piety and humility. It so happened once that an unmarried girl from his neighborhood got big with child. When questioned by her parents, she did not disclose the name of the real culprit due to fear but named the monk as the father of the unborn child. Enraged, the parents minced no words and lambasted the monk severely. Hakuin Zenji neither refuted nor accepted the allegation. "Is that so?" was all he reiterated again and again.

When the child saw the light of the day, it was brought to Hakuin Zenji. The monk now had to find food for two, though in the wake of his soiled reputation, he, many a times, received more barbs than food. By the time the year was out, the girl-mother could stand it no longer and revealed the identity of her lover, a fish market help, to her parents. The parents apologized to the monk, repeatedly begged his forgiveness and the custody of the child. The sage handed over the child to them, mumbling a whisper: "Is that so?" Promptly the sage went back to his meditative posture.

Innocence is neither defensive nor offensive, neither reactive nor proactive. When first the monk said, "Is that so?", he 'perhaps meant: "Is this what these people believe?" As he was aware of who he was, he was like an alien to their belief system. He didn't depend upon their opinion to define him. To him the charges were irrelevant off scorings that called for no response either in yes or no. While his reputation played see-saw, he turned around and spoke to **existence (God)**: "Is that so?" A man of piety owes his allegiance only to existence.

When the child was brought to him, he took yet another existential dispensation. A sage does not question anything dished out to him by existence. Any hesitation would be tantamount to a disregard of existence. Some people would call such an attitude as "choicelessness" but a sage does not choose even "choicelessness" because that would mean losing his inner dynamics, his inner balance. In Zazen Wasan,(Hakuin Zenji's song in praise of zazen), he sings: "We stand beyond ego and past clever words then the gate to oneness of cause-and-effect is thrown open". What the child needed immediately was a' father's love and protection and not the gossip of idle village folks. Being in present was his métier. And so he baby-sat the child till the day he was asked to part with it. Did he not develop any bond with the child? We don't know. We only know that he remained routed in the fulcrum of his inner balance. For him depth of living was more meaningful than any length of living. For length we scour the past and the future but depth happens in the present. There was no knee-jerk action from him, only a lover's plaint to existence:

"Is that so?" that is to say, what is this joke, now?

The sound of one hand clapping is a beautiful gift of Hakuin Zenji to Zen. We, who bobble in the ambit of bubble chambers created and sustained by a ceaseless flow of frivolous thoughts, would do well to work on it to get a glimpse of Hakuin Zenji's envious, yet accomplish-able, state. All the time the sage was talking to God or the Force and not really to those who were troubling him.

Man has many desires. God alone possesses the ability to fulfill them. When his desires are not fulfilled, he feels utterly miserable. Although there is infinite potential in each one of us, we cannot attain all of our desires due to our own **Self-imposed limitations**. At such times, what can man do to remove his limitations and achieve his goals? Of all methods of self-development, prayer is considered the simplest and the most effective.

Prayer (Ardas)

Many people pray, but few truly know the efficacy of prayer or how to pray. Prayer is generally misunderstood to be a charge sheet of complaints against God, or a shopping list of desires. Indeed, often our prayers are nothing more than sheer beggary.

So, what exactly is prayer? When we are unable to do something on our own, we pray in an attempt to tune in to some Higher Power. When we surrender in devotion at the altar of the All Knowing, the All Powerful and the All Compassionate, we liquidate our limited ego and the power of the Higher flows through us and helps us achieve that which seems difficult or impossible. This is the principle of **invocation**.

The universe is a cosmos not chaos. People may not believe in religion or theories of God. Even so, many people do feel that some Higher Power pulsates through, and guides the universe. Attune yourself to this Higher Power in whatever way you can, and visualize whatever form you like - whatever gives you peace, a sense of divinity and encouragement in your heart.

There are five essential steps in any prayer. The first is **Naman (prostration)**. To prostrate is to have an attitude of humility. If we have to ask the Lord for something, then it must be done with humility. Very often, we approach the Lord with one of our many prides. Of these, the pride of the intellect is the most dangerous. Wealth, power and beauty come and go, but he who is proud of his intellect is never ready to accept his own Ignorance, and thus remains proud and arrogant forever.

The second step is **Simaran (invoking)**. This is to invoke the presence of the Lord in our mind or in the heart. For that Higher is not merely an idol, symbol or concept. That is a living reality, the Absolute Truth. Call the Lord with love to listen to your prayer.

The **third step is Kirtan (praise)**. Praise is never for the Lord. He does not need it. But it is only when we praise or revere' someone that we are capable of surrendering our ego. It is only when we surrender our ego at the altar of love and respect that His divinity flows through us.

The fourth step is **Yaachana (asking of boons)**. We should first invoke the Lord's presence, praise Him and then ask Him for what we need. Ask not merely for things. Ask for strength intelligence and knowledge. With only strength, we are unable to achieve much. Intelligence is also necessary. And without the right knowledge, the intellect is of little use. Ask for His blessings and His lotus feet. Having got these by the grace of the Lord - need one asks for more?

The fifth step is **Arpan (surrender)**. Now that we have asked something of the Lord, should we not offer Him something in return? But what could we possibly offer the Lord that he does not already have? We should offer what we have in plenty, and that which God has none. These are the five kaleshas and the six vikaras. The **kaleshas are all the miseries caused by ignorance, likes, dislikes, fear of death and the ego.** The **vikaras are the six poisons of the mind, which cause agitation -lust, anger, greed, attachment, arrogance and jealousy.** Offer all these so that the Lord can take them away from you.

Thus, in the process of praying, we should prostrate in all humility (naman), invoke the Higher Power that flows through the universe (simaran) and sing the glories of the Lord (kirtan). While surrendering our many weaknesses (arpan), we may ask for our boons (yaachana).

This brings us to a question that what boon should be asked for? Any worldly substance or favor requested would amount to interference with the path, which He has chalked out for us. He may grant the boon but then one is on a path chosen by oneself (Manmukhi) resulting in unforeseen difficulties.

Remember that prayer is not only for asking for something. No gain is a gain until and unless we recognize what we have and what we have gained. Prayer should also be out of our sense of appreciation and gratitude for what ever He has given us.

Through prayer one must seek His blessings His continues protection and ability to meditate and serve Him.

Normally we ask for our pains (Dhuk) to be condoned. This is akin to treatment based on symptoms only. For example if one is suffering from Malaria, one cannot be treated by paracetamol or tynol alone. Basic drug like chloroquine would be required to eradicate the basic cause of the fever. Our pains arise out of our deeds of the past. We must seek pardon of the deeds to be free from the pain. Merely praying does not guarantee pardon. One has to repent (*prayaschit*). This is where the guide is helpful since he is able to see the past and future and assign punishments like service and Simran. Thereafter, based on his recommendations ones sins can be pardoned and destiny changed.

Should we pray for others? We find a priest praying for us in temples and other religious places. The clergy without their involvement does that. They take money and convey one' wishes to God which actually means nothing. If some one prays for another person then either he takes upon the problems on to himself or donates some part of his accumulated meditation. When such a prayer is done by a realized soul then God listens because prayer by such a person would only be after considering all angles.

The recommendations of such a person seldom go unheard. The guide one chooses, if done carefully, would have vast meditation accumulated in his account. So granting a portion of it would by like donating a bucket of water from a mighty river. A person who has very little credit in terms of meditation can loose the credit by praying for others or cursing people through ego. Also one does not have ability to understand if a person is genuinely attached to God or undergoing punishment or a fake. So praying for him may be constituted, as interference with what God wants.

Prayer by Sangat or the entire community is a concept peculiar to Sikhism. Here the prayer (Ardas) is done with all devotees present, which is like signing the petition. This can be effective provided devotees are genuinely praying from their heart and not simply looking at their watches as to when it will be over and they can go to have Lungar (community feast). If granted by Lord it may change the laid out path by Him, which again will mean that the individual is on his own.

An example will clarify. Many individuals ask for a child. They pray hard, ask many saints who may not be realized souls but just masquerading. They may get what they want but the child may turn out to be unhealthy or a sinful personality. On the other hand if prayer is through a realized soul who would know future and past the soul send as a child may be appropriate to the deserving parents. That child may grow up as an asset to the family.

Recommendation for beginners is that never pray for others because one does not know what God wants. When the Guru or the Guide gives one power to pray after discerning if the person deserves or not then only one should pray for selected few.

This brings us to a basic question that do we wait for purity of mind before we start to meditate or we go ahead without waiting?

We shall examine this aspect in the next chapter.

෴ ෴ ෴

CHAPTER FIVE

PURITY OF MIND

Should one meditate only if the mind is pure or meditation itself purifies the mind is a question which haunts most of meditators. A simple answer would be that meditation helps in purifying the mind as well as in achieving the final objects. To understand this concept in-depth analysis is required.

Ancient scriptures mention that one should be free from ten faults to meditate as well as to gain from the power of mantras. A holy dip in the river Ganges is supposed to free a person from these ten faults. The day Ganges was born is called *Dashara* meaning the day, which removes these faults. This day is the Tenth day of waxing moon (increasing). As we discussed in the proceeding chapter, faults cannot be just washed away without penance. These faults (Dosh) are as follows: -

1. Criticism of a saint or Rishi.
2. Non-believer in God- Nastik.
3. No faith in surti or Naam recitation of God's name.
4. No faith in the word of Guru.
5. Differentiating between Vishnu and Shiva.
6. While reciting lacks concentration.
7. Reciting wrong names.
8. Does not espouse naam.

9. Does not follow righteous path
10. Has no faith on scriptures.

However, waiting for becoming fault free will imply endless wait. As one progresses slowly purity of mind will be achieved. These faults are more for recitation mantras effectively than for meditation or attainment. It will be clear from the example below.

When Mahmoud Gazni invaded Somnath temple, Brahmins told the rulers that they would be able to protect the temple by chanting mantras, which would invoke power of the gods. However, nothing happened while the invader had a field day. This was because those who chanted the mantras were NOT free from these ten faults. When a pundit is called for by anyone for knowing the future, invariably he tells about problems ahead and recommends Hawan or puja or jaap extra, which he would do on one's behalf. Invariable it does not change the situation because the Pundit is NOT free from these faults. Thus all activities performed by him are null and void. From meditation point of view purity of mind would imply following qualities embedded in the mind: -

• **Compassion.** This quality is not pity but a quality of heart. It means caring for others in all ways. Sometimes it may involve mild scolding or asking some one to do hard work which may not be to the liking of that person. Still one may insist that the person does something, which would put him on the righteous path. It could involve invoking artificial anger at times. Pity on the other hand means to help the other person to ride over a problem or assist a person monetarily or by providing subsidy.

- **Speech**. A meditator must be soft spoken without getting angry. He should always speak the truth. In rare cases if it helps a needy person, truth may be camouflaged. It is a very difficult decision to make whether to speak the truth in such cases. Therefore, beginners are not advised to get involved in such situations otherwise they may cross boundaries. It is very difficult for an ordinary person to judge who is needy or who is undergoing punishment for his sins or who is only trying to gain some advantage for his personal gain. At Bhuchon Kalan (near Bathinda) a devotee had been bestowed with powers to revive any dead person. While passing through a village he was moved by the grief of a dead person's dear and near ones. He could not withstand that so he revived that person. His Guru was annoyed with him and withdrew powers given to him. It is not easy to stick to truth in all situations. Once a person gets in the habit of speaking truth always then it becomes easy. However, one has to link speaking truth to the fear, which we discussed in the proceeding chapter. One who owes allegiance to God is fearless, as he knows that God is on his side. Situation where truth is camouflaged by realized souls is best understood by a true story dating back to Guru Arjan Devji's times. One of His disciples was meditating near a pond. Bidhi Chand was a thief who used to rob buffalos and other animals of the villagers. At night, he untied some buffalos but the villagers were alert and chased him when he took them away. When he reached the pond where the disciple was meditating, he caught the feet of the disciple and asked for protection. The disciple told him to think about Guru Arjan Devji and ask for protection. He also told Bhidi Chandji to sit next to him and meditate. The buffalos in the mean time went into the pond. When the villagers came and asked the disciple if he had seen a thief with the buffalos, he denied having seen any body. He told them that there are some buffalos in the pond. The villagers looked towards the pond and said that their buffalos were black in color while these are brownish in color. Thereafter they went in another direction only to return empty handed. Guru Arjan Devji had some how made the villagers believe that the buffalos in the pond were not theirs. Bhidi Chandji was a changed person from that day onwards moving on to become one of the ardent disciples of the Guru. The buffalos returned to their homes in the morning. Such situations can be handled only by realized souls. Listening to explanations (katha) gives lot of knowledge provided the explanations are given by a realized soul. Normal clergy give their views with a bias and with an eye on the basket where donations are kept. If a person does not tell a single lie for twelve years then what ever he says will happen. This power is difficult to obtain. It can be obtained through meditation also but it can create difficulties especially for armatures. Sometimes inadvertently one says something then it may happen which cannot be undone easily. It can happen even with those who have reached the highest level.

• When Guru Nanakdev Ji declared Guru Angad Dev Ji as His successor, Guru Nanakdev Ji said that from then onwards Guru Angad Dev Ji will be the Guru. Saying this he bowed down and touched the feet of Guru Angad Dev Ji with his forehead, which surprised the Second Guru. Guru Angad Dev Ji inadvertently said, "Oh God! I should have leprosy on my feet which have caused my Guru to bow down." Now that had to happen. Guru Nanakdev Ji said that he cannot undo what the Second Guru has said but he would restrict it to only one inner most toe. Thereafter, pus used to flow from Guru Angad Dev Ji's toe. Guru Amardas Ji was so dedicated that he used to swallow the pus. This flow of pus was passed on to the Third Guru, Guru Amardas Ji, then onto the Fourth Guru, Guru Ramdas Ji and then to Guru Arjan Dev Ji, the fifth Guru. While Guru Arjan Dev Ji was composing Sukhmani Sahib when he finished the Sixteenth Astpadi, a thought came to His mind. He thought that Sukhmani Sahib if recited properly can cure any disease but if the pus continues to flow from His own toe then how will anyone have faith. So he went to meet Baba Srichand Ji, elder son of Guru Nanakdev Ji at Pathankot. He explained to Him what he was doing and also told Him about the thought which had come to His mind. Babaji told Him to add the slok recited by His Holy father. This was done with a little modification, as Guru Arjan Dev Ji did not want to be a competitor of the First Guru. Babaji also Condoned the utterance of Guru Angad Dev Ji so that the pus stops flowing. Therefore, if a person ever gets to the stage where what ever he says will happen, he has to exercise lot of care and speak only bare minimum. In addition sometimes when such people say something, which is not in the path, chalked out by the God then it is construed as interference with His ways.

- **Righteous Path**. A meditator must always follow righteous path no matter what difficulties he may face. Some times God or the Guru sows obstacles just to test a person. Once a person negotiates them successfully then only he can progress further.
- **Detached From material Substances**. It implies detachment from what is called 'Maya', which has two connotations. First are **monetary benefits** and second is **lust for sex**. Both are important for existence because without money one cannot live and without the other humanity cannot grow. If someone goes to the forest after giving up worldly pleasures, he would

still require food for which he may have to depend on alms. If one accepts alms then one has to pay back either in this birth or the next one, which is akin to taking a loan. Without sex the humanity will end. Many of those who go to forest for meditation are unable to get over their lust which erupts when opportunity presents itself. During ancient times we find a lot of rishis being lured by the gods like Indra who felt threatened due to their meditation. Therefore, Guru Nanak Devji has chalked out an easier path by recommending that one should be in this world, earn in a righteous manner without getting attached to monetary or power benefits. Examples quoted are of the lotus flower in a pond and of the ducks, which take care not to wet their wings while floating in the water. Islam recommends 2.5 percent of ones income to be donated while Sikhism calls for Ten percent donations. This money has to be donated for charity where it can be put to the purpose it is meant for. Organizations which may put the funds so collected to other uses, should be avoided since such donations are NOT accepted by God. As far as lust is concerned one wife one husband is recommended by Guru Nanak Devji. All others should be treated as brothers, sisters, or mothers and fathers.

- **Humility.** Bhai Nandlal ji during Guru Gobind Singhji's times saw the Guru in all human beings. Similarly as a meditator progresses, he recognizes the element of God in all. Thus he considers himself as the lowest beings. He considers himself at par with the dust of the feet of all. We also have examples of devotees (Bhagats) running after a dog to give it buttered bread. Guru Nanak Devji always addressed Himself as the lowest being setting an example of humility.
- **Santosh (Satisfaction).** Unless one feels satisfied with what ever has been to him by Almighty, greed will never leave that

person. The Eastern thought propagates satisfaction to progress towards final goal of salvation. There is no end to materialistic gains because whatever one may get it would, never be sufficient unless one feel that it is. Some feel that it is an impediment to progress but that is not true. Our ancient scriptures bear testimony of the knowledge, which was possessed by the intellectuals of that time. Reason why the knowledge did not spread is because they were not willing to share it with others. It was passed on from father to son, which implied that it got lost after some generations. On the other hand the knowledge flowed freely in the Western society, which is responsible for materialistic progress. Other reason for their being materialistic is their attachment to their body, which requires comforts. It is imperative that those who meditate develop *santosh*.

Guru NanakdevJi in 38th Stanza of Japji Sahib has stated that seven virtues are required to be developed as under:-

1. Self Control. Control over all our Senses (*Indiriyas*)
2. Patience. (*Santosh*)
3. Understanding like the anvil
4. Spiritual wisdom
5. Love of God
6. Strengthen your body with inner heat to shape as per His desires
7. In the crucible of love melt the nectar of Naam and mint the true coin of the sabad, the word of God.

Penance or repenting does not imply that one calls a clergyman, gives him money on a promise that he would chant some mantras, which will free the person from a sin. Alternately bathing in holy waters by itself does not make a person sin- free. Penance has following ramifications: -

- Genuinely feeling sorry for what has been done.
- Promise not to commit such an act in the future.
- Damage control of those who have been harmed because of the act.
- Undergoing the punishment, which has been prescribed by the Guru. It can be in the form of service, recitation of naam, donation at a place where it would be utilized for the purpose it is meant for.
- Apology thus also involves a role-reversal: the person apologizing relinquishes power and puts himself at the mercy of the offended party who may or may not credit the apology. Thus it is in the hands of the Guru to accept or reject the apology.

Having seen what qualities need to be developed, we would have a look at the habits or qualities, which have to be got rid off. Meditation itself helps in the process though the meditator is required to make a concentric effort.

- **Desires**. There is no end to desires. All materialistic desires (Kamna) should be shelved. When one puts oneself in the hands of God, He gives that person what ever is needed. If the person wants to run a free Kitchen (Lungar) then God would give him the resources required. How, when and where should be left to Him.
- **Anger**. If someone has a desire it is either fulfilled or it is not. If it is fulfilled then greed sets in but if it is not fulfilled then anger takes its place. Controlling anger we will deal separately later on.

- **Greed**. This is the root cause of many ills. Asking for more and more of something, which is not required, is greed. If it involves depriving of someone else then its implications increase many folds.
- **Love for the near and dear ones (MOH)**. WE all have our family towards which we all have our responsibilities to discharge. However, excessive attachment towards it constitutes moh, which has to be avoided.
- **Ego (Ahemkar)**. This is a disease of the soul. It should be avoided at all costs. We will deal with it separately.
- **Jealousy and hatred**. We will deal with important aspect later.
- **Fear**. A meditator does not fear any body. He only loves God.
- **Have No enemies**.

God- Guru- Saint – self Alignment.

This alignment is typically an Eastern thought. Teacher (Guru) and student (Chela) relationship has been brought out in our book on *Motivation; Theory of Prerna*. To realize God, one must have a path indicator. Guru guides us how to reach there. Guru can be actually a form of God like all primordial or gods like Brahma, Vishnu or Lord Shiva or any other god. However, we pray to them and act on their teachings but until we reach a stage where they regularly give us visions it is difficult to follow them unless there is a guide in human form who is way ahead of us which means a saint. In modern times it is very difficult to find one such true saint since many greedy people pretend to be saints. Signs of a true saint are defined in Eighth and Ninth Ashtpadi of Sukhmani Sahib in Sri Guru Granth Sahib. Saints may be followers of any religion as they are **realized souls**. However, they are not to be mixed up with **clergy** who may or may not be true saints. During ancient times many people searched for a stone known as Paras (**philosopher's stone**) which if touches a metal could turn into gold. Guru or a saint is such a paras who turns his followers not only into gold but also into paras; means turns them into like himself with similar powers. Thus true saint is one who aligns people with God by giving them support while a false saint is one who aligns a person to him using the name of God. This litmus paper test can help us to find a true guide. A person must align himself with the Guide- Guru-God. Unless one can identify presence of God in the guide and the Guru attainment is difficult.

One should never test a true Guide or Guru. To be sure if he is true Guide or not, just go to His congregation and take a back seat. If he is a true saint then He would himself call you and tell everything about you past and future and what sins or good deeds have been committed by you.

A true saint near Bhuchokalan near Bathinda, was meditating sitting under a bush in the month of June which is the hottest month in India. A shepherd who had goats, used to give him milk daily. One day he asked the saint as to how the Saint could sit in that heat and meditate. The saint told him that he could also do it. If he wished to try, then he should come early in the morning at six and experiment. Next day the shepherd came. The saint told him to sit under another bush and start reciting Naam. Next the shepherd opened his eyes when it was six in the evening. From that day onwards he was blessed. Thus if the Guru-guide is pleased realization can come in minutes. Above incident brings out that first of all a person has to be a seeker (Gyasu). Once he has quest for achieving final objective, then he has to make an effort to achieve it. If he takes one step then God will come forward taking thousand steps. Here the shepherd had quest for knowledge and had taken the first step by coming at six in the morning knowing fully well that the day is going to be very hot. Thereafter, the Guru/Guide had by recommendation or by His own powers helped him to concentrate to meditate whole day in the state of being oblivion to the surroundings. After spending one day in this state there is no looking back. This is how a guide can help to achieve something in minutes, which may take years otherwise.

A person working in GREF (Border roads construction organization) was admitted in Srinagar Military hospital since he was very sick almost on the verge of dying. The doctors gave up hope. Just before he died he prayed to Guru Gobind Singh Ji. He had vision of a saint immediately after that. There after, he died and felt that he is away from his body. The doctors declared him dead but did not move his body to the mortuary because it was nighttime. They simply moved his bed to a corner and covered his face and body with bed sheet. After about an hour or so he got up. Everybody around was surprised as well as frightened. Nurse came running, doctor was called. They examined him and found him to be absolutely fit. He was duly discharged from the hospital to get back to work. After some time he retired and settled down in Ferozepur. All the time he kept wondering who the saint was. All he remembered was the Saint's image and words "Sat Kartar". One day a person who was a devotee of the Saint came to his house. He told him about the whereabouts of the Saint. When he went for His darshan, the Saint told him that he was tasked by Guru Sahib to revive him. Such is the power of realized souls.

❧ ❧ ❧

CHAPTER SIX

DEVELOPMENT OF VIRTUES AND WEEDING OUT OF VICES JEALOUSY AND HATRED

༄༺༒༻༄

Jealousy and hatred cannot exist without each other. Together they are one of the most destructive forces. Hatred manifests itself in the form of attitudes and behavior, while jealousy remains hidden but provides impetus to hatred for creating destruction.

As per Sai Baba, there are a number of important signs of jealousy. **Jealousy makes its appearance when one meets a person who has earned greater fame than one.** Or it will develop when a person has more wealth than oneself. Jealousy will also show its head when one comes into the presence of a person who is more beautiful and handsome. For students, jealousy will soon appear if there is another student who scores higher marks than self. **It is the weakness of ordinary human beings to develop jealousy whenever they come in contact with people who excel them in terms of wealth, position, beauty, intelligence, and other such qualities.**

Jealousy will not live harmlessly inside a person. The moment jealousy enters all the virtues, which have been cultivated over a long time, all the great qualities which have been developed, are destroyed. It ruins the human nature; **it strengthens the animal nature**; it promotes the demonic nature. **It has no scruples**. It does not look forward or backward. It is such an insidious quality that one must see to it that jealousy will never possess oneself.

Enjoy the prosperity of others. Enjoy the progress of others. Enjoy the welfare of others.

Enjoy the beauty of others. This is true virtue. This is one of the most important teachings of the Bhagwat *Gita*. **Desiring the good of others is a laudable quality which everyone should possess."**

The stress caused due to these twin qualities can take enormous form. Question arises what gives rise to these two twin sisters? It is ego, which boosts them. One can have ego problems even with God where one may consider that everything is being done oneself and God has nothing to do. History is replete with examples where ego takes gigantic forms. Spirituality accompanied with egoism, jealousy and hatred is a deadly combination. A person can be destroyed beyond repairs as given in "Vaar" of Gauri Raag in the GURU GRANTH SAHIB. NEVER Misuse your powers to curse. Also it is for consideration that anyone who does jantra- mantra (Black magic) to harm others cannot sit in front of GURU Granth Sahib even for five minutes.

Sai Baba Says, "You become wise when you become fragrant with virtues. But if you are saturated with bad qualities, with doubts and all sorts of jealousy and hatred, you will not be able to understand anything at all. That is why it has been said, *'Death is sweeter than the blindness of ignorance.'* one must free oneself from ignorance. Jealousy is an evil, which develops that ignorance. Therefore, students who have very tender hearts, who have a bright future ahead of them and much progress to make, should never give room to jealousy. If any person in someone's class gets an outstanding grade one should not succumb to jealousy.

One can also work to attain an outstanding grade. If one has not achieved that and one also feel jealous, thereby making **two mistakes**. In the first place, one has not studied adequately, otherwise one would have done better; and in the second place, one has darkened the heart with jealousy. Then crying over it is the **third mistake**. One should not develop these bad qualities which are sure to cause oneself so much trouble; they can even destroy a whole family which may have been previously happy and enjoying all the goodness of life.

Jealousy and Hatred destroy those who possess them

While explaining these principles to Arjuna, Krishna told Arjuna, "For your evil cousins, the one hundred brothers who have been plotting to destroy the Pandavas' joy and happiness, it is their evil qualities which encouraged them to do all their wicked deeds. **People who are jealous attract bad people for company.** These cousins have with them their evil uncle, who encouraged them in their enmity towards the Pandavas. He is filled with jealousy.

Patience, Forbearance and Love are virtues, which can overcome jealousy and hatred. One who is jealous will continue to criticize the other hoping for a reaction, but if there were no reaction from the receiver then automatically it would die down. Love of Second degree, involving sacrifice can destroy these two evils."

Negativity

Negativity is felt in the atmosphere due to negative thinking. **"When we feel angry or fearful, very subtle chemicals are emitted by our bodies. They are called pheromones. They enter the atmosphere in incredibly small concentrations, but our sense of smell detects them, recognizes the fear chemicals or the anger chemicals, and sends the message straight to the primitive brain centers where your own "fight or flight" mechanism is initiated.**

Colloquialisms such as "tension in the air," "gut feeling," and "I smell a rat" all have a physiological basis" Dr. Paul Skye in Off Loading Stress.

That is why when someone thinks negatively about others or someone is thinking negatively about anyone, then first of all pressure is felt at the nose where while breathing these particles accumulate; one feels like tickling one's nose. As per Eastern Philosophy we should praise only the Lord and criticize ourselves only. There is no room for any third person in between. Western thought process also mentions self-serving bias because of which we criticize others and attribute all errors to others rather than self. This kind of attitude causes lot of stress distracting a person who is meditating.

Revenge. Feeling of revenge is responsible for many sins, which are committed, wastage of time and resources and destruction, which may result. Feeling of revenge at national level leads to unnecessary wars. A person who meditates knows that everything that happens is due to His will. God makes someone as a medium through whom He acts. Therefore, for him all are acts of God, which implies that revenge has no place in his curriculum. If someone has harmed the person in question then the decision to punish the offender is left to God. May be in previous births that person may have been harmed by the person in question. If that were not the case then God would square it up.

HOW TO CONTROL ANGER

Western Thoughts

Anger is an emotion, which is negative in nature. Therefore, it is five times more powerful than positive emotions like happiness. It can lead to violence if sufficient stress has accumulated, trigger is available and a weapon is handy. Frustrations results out of denial of something, which we want; this in turn gives rise to anger. It is intense feeling directed at someone. When it is directed at self, then it can turn inwards leading to suicide. Another factor is tolerance of others. Tolerance also varies as per degree of non-tolerance. First stage is strong likes and dislikes. The second stage is dismissing and third stage is disapproval. These stages give rise to different stages of anger.

Remedies for anger in the Western philosophy focuses on exercising control and restrain. How much one gets angry will depend upon Emotional Intelligence, which includes emotional coaching and Laissez fare. Emotional labor is advocated.

Eastern Thoughts

Emotions as per eastern thoughts are only two namely; pleasure and displeasure. These stem from desires as it is Kamna (desire), which gives rise to pleasure if fulfilled and if it is not then one is displeased. When desire is fulfilled then one asks for more hence greed is born and one gains confidence which gradually turns into ego. If the desire is not fulfilled then one gets angry. Since failure is mostly attributed to external causes one gets angry with others. In case it is directed towards self then depression would result.

• Thus everything revolves around state of mind, which is responsible for attitude and behavior. Logically the mind should be under control of brain (logical thinking) and soul (Atma) but practically it runs free and controls the person. Does it mean that all desires are bad? The simple answer would be NO because if that happens this world will stop functioning and person will lose his or her identity. Eastern religions provide various safeguards for genuine and healthy desires; for example Hinduism provides for four Ashrams while Sikhism states that one need not renounce the world and still obtain salvation. Question then arise how much is too much which can be termed as greed? Whatever is essential for one's living is not greed. The essential and comfort level for each will differ as per status and requirement. More than that for accumulation is the greed, which would not be bounded by any limits. Another measure is what is rightfully yours should be given to you but to obtain something at the cost of others or by giving pain to others is greed. Guru Har Rai Ji the Seventh Guru of Sikhs while answering Sangat's (followers) questions said that greed was the root cause of all sins. 85% of Bill Gates' income goes into charity, which is commendable and shows lack of greed. Thus anger is closely linked to desires and state of mind with ego playing a major part. A person who is Gurmukh (goes by what God says or does and accepts His doings) will not get angry while others will. Repeated anger would intensify hatred towards others giving rise to jealousy. Also effect of anger is on thinking where brain is affected and stops thinking rationally. About mind this is what the Upnishads (ancient Indian scriptures) have to say: -

"My mind did not see; my mind was elsewhere. I did not see or hear; for a man sees and hears with his mind" Brihadaranyaka Upinishad, 1-v-3.

Two violent passions are hatred and malice, which can be eradicated by love, compassion and sympathy. Hatred answered by hatred will only add fuel to the fire because two negatives do not make positive instead they add to make double negative.

Fear

There is only one type of fear that is the **fear of people**. One may examine this in detail and conclusion will be the same. If one is nearing death then worry is what will happen to one's family. Further all fear is in the mind only. There is a famous story about Nick, a worker who along with other workers was celebrating birthday of the foreman. In the end of the day he was somehow left alone in the refrigerated room. He knocked, tried all walls and floor to get out, shouted and did his utmost to get help. No one was around hence he died by morning; frozen to death. In the morning when his body was being taken for postmortem all were standing in grief. However, most amazing thing was that the room was NEVER LOCKED. It was all his imagination and perception, which means **panic**. We should maintain our cool so that solutions come by. During crisis it is essential to remain cool while before crisis bit of stress actually helps to improve performance.

Causes of Anger

Having considered both the thought processes, let us see what exactly causes anger. There are number of causes, some related to each other while others independent of others. These are discussed below not strictly in any order but at random.

- There are number of persons with higher Intelligence Quotient (IQ). Average being hundred they may have up to one hundred and thirty or more. They think very fast and can plan many steps ahead while others with average IQ cannot. Net result is frustration with their slow understanding and functioning, which can escalate to anger. This kind of people are generally not team workers as they find others are not up to standard; hence they can be troublesome.
- Another cause is when one has life position "I am NOT OK". In such cases one is frustrated with self and gets irritated very fast. Such people lack confidence and may be introvert. Outwardly they may put up false front in the form of anger. This kind of anger can be directed outward or inward towards self; in both cases it is bound to create stress. Since these life positions develop early in life, lot depends on environment during child hood. A child brought up in too much of controlled atmosphere can revolt or feel that he is not OK while others are superior.

- Those who have position "You are NOT OK". They feel that most people are useless and do not want to work unless forced to. They work from what is known as Macgregor's X Theory; hence they get annoyed very fast. This position is developed during childhood when the child judges others and finds that there is lot of difference in what they profess and what they do. For example parents tell children never to tell lies which the child wants to abide by. Then one day when the phone rings the child picks up but the parents do not want to talk to the caller. So they tell the child to say that the parent was not at home. The child gets a message that there is something wrong. Even innocuous things like when child is ready to jump from a table we say, "do not jump otherwise you will get hurt". The child ignores it and jumps but does not get hurt since 90 % chances are that nothing will happen. The parents have said about getting hurt because they know that there is a chance of getting hurt and consequences are severe, but the child's experience tells the child that the parents were wrong. Such things repeatedly occurring will give a message that "you are not OK".

- When the child is angry with one parent specially the opposite sex parent then also anger develops. Sulking also results from such situations where when the child grows up plays psychological games.

- Strokes, which we receive during childhood, also contribute towards anger. Positive strokes help to reduce anger while negative or mixed will increase it.

- Desires specially ambition when it does not match with capabilities or circumstances results in anger.

- Basic value system is very important. If one believes in God the chances of getting annoyed are less. Also belief in luck plays a major role.

- Lack of tolerance of ambiguity or tolerance of others contributes to anger substantially.

Remedies

Situational Approach. Western philosophy advocates Emotional labor approach to hide one's emotions while dealing with people where getting emotional can be harmful to one's cause. This approach has a serious problem as hiding emotions would mean that they are turned inwards causing stress which when accumulates can be harmful. As against this approach, Armed forces follow situational approach where each situation, which can arise, is discussed, planned and training carried out to deal with it. Take the example of firing by the enemy or an ambush laid by insurgents. When such a situation arises getting emotional can only happen in the movies. On ground one has to think clearly, take action and deal with the situation in a professional manner. Let us examine daily routine of a busy CEO of a company. One morning he may find customers irritated with whom he has to deal politely, and then he finds a worker not doing his job whom he has to say few things sternly. Thereafter, when he comes back to office there may be someone who has worked extremely well who has to be rewarded and then a clerk may have made a mistake who has to be perhaps fired and then give further directions to someone. May be he has to end the day with a meeting of board of directors. Such a person will never have anger otherwise he just cannot function. While scolding he may have to put up a front then smile when rewarding another person. For him these are just situations requiring standard response and then get back home where children are waiting.

Even while dealing with children at times we have to put up a front without actually getting annoyed. When one is actually angry one should avoid action. There was a parent whose child was sober but when instigated could get a bit troublesome inviting complaints. The parent knew this and would always deal patiently with him rather than getting violent. When things were going out of hand then both parents would decide that time has come when the child requires a bit of dressing down. The father would wait for the child to return from school then would scold him as required, reason it out with him and after that forget about it and behave normal. Such children would grow into confident person with I am OK – You are OK position.

Baba Sheik Faridji in SGGS aptly brings out Key to Good health in relation to control of anger. "Answer evil with goodness; do not fill your mind with anger. Your body shall not suffer from any disease and you shall obtain everything."

EGO (AHAMKAR)

Ego is mother of all vices and sins. SGGS describes ego as a disease of the soul. Rest is all Dukh (miseries or grief or sufferings). Miseries or sufferings are those, which we undergo due to our past deeds. These are of **four types**. Firstly birth and death itself is suffering which we want to get over by meditation. Second are those which arise due to problems with are body. These we generally term as diseases. Third are those, which we face due to monetary problems and greed. Fourth are those, which arise due to Moh (love of near and dear ones). All of these are result of our deeds of which we may be aware or may not especially if they are of the past lives. We get worried and start asking in prayer to save us from the misery. Sometimes God agrees but the sin stands which manifests in another misery resulting in more prayers. Thus to remove the root cause, we have to do service, recite naam and meditate. Such actions will reduce the effect of miseries as well as give us strength to bear them by remaining in permanent bliss.

Getting back to ego, we find that ego is a disease which if not cured will effect meditation adversely. If we believe that every thing in nature is being done by God either directly or through all of us, then considering oneself as the doer would mean that one is contemporary of God. It also goes against the principle of humility (Nimarta). We become proud of our very small achievements and are ever willing to project ourselves as a person who does no wrong being better than others. A meditator should consider himself as the lowest of all beings while the Guru, Guide and God as above all. The path of meditation is like the game of snakes and ladders. One progresses slowly as per dice. Then the Guide and the Guru may shower blessings, which act like ladders. If ego sets in at any stage it acts like the snakes. The worst snake is the one whose mouth is at 97 or 98 (Just short of the final goal). It brings a player back to the count of two or three. This snake is similar to the ego of a meditator who has acquired number of powers by meditating for many births but becomes proud of his meditation. This kind of ego brings the meditator back to from where he started.

The lowest gains from meditation are monetary gains. Next is power due to politics or position which one holds. The highest powers are the ones, which stem from meditation. Ego, which results from such powers bring down the person on the same scale, which implies that downfall, would be rapid if one has spiritual powers. SGGS says, "First agree to die and become dust of the feet of everyone, then come to God for achievement." It implies that a meditator should kill his ego and consider himself as the dust of the feet of all before meditation takes affect.

There is another type of ego, which requires to be avoided. Sometimes when one is reciting naam or normal banies or reading Holy Scriptures, mind races to far away places. Invariably past incidents where one has done well come to mind instead of incidents where one has failed or remained humble. Such situations should be avoided specially when one is meditating or saying one's prayers.

Relinquishing of ego implies giving up **criticism** of all. Criticism of saints or listening to such criticism in particular can be very harmful because even God does not pardon such people. Only the saint whose criticism is in question can pardon such an act. Criticism of God can be pardoned once recommended by a saint, but God does not pardon criticism of a saint. It is very difficult to recognize who is a true saint or is a fake. Sometimes true saints also entice devotees with money and pretend to be a fake to ward off those who are not true followers. In any case a meditator should praise only the LORD and restrict criticism to only that of self.

One story of ancient times and one of recent times would demonstrate the concept. King Prikshat fasted on Ekadeshi (eleventh day of rising Moon). Rishi Durwasa came there with his followers and desired that they have food together after the fast time would be over. Before that he proceeded to bathe in the river. When the time to break the fast approached, the king became anxious as the Rishi was nowhere in sight. He then took some water and decided to wait for the Rishi for food. When the Rishi arrived after his bath and came to know that the king had taken a sip of water, he became angry and decided to curse the king. Since the King was a devotee and was known for his saintly qualities, Lord Vishnu was annoyed thus releasing his weapon "Surdashna Chakra" to harm the Rishi. When the Rishi saw the weapon, he ran to escape from it. He went all over the universe but the weapon kept following him. He even went to the abode of Lord Vishnu and asked him to recall his weapon. Lord Vishnu refused by saying that only person who can pardon him is the King himself. Thus Rishi Durwasa had to go back to the king and ask for pardon, which was duly granted by the humble king. Lord Vishnu recalled the weapon.

Second true incident occurred in 1930s at Buchokalan, near Bathinda (Punjab). An overseer (Class two officer) of irrigation department came to *Romi Dera* and criticized a well-known saint. Even after repeated requests the overseer seemed adamant and moved towards the door to leave saying that he would not spare anyone.

Before the overseer could leave his body was paralyzed. Some people took him to his home. Thereafter, his family went all over to seek pardon including to the saint in question. The saint said that if the overseer had criticized him he would not have harmed him but he cannot undo what ever His Guru has done. The Overseer had to undergo full cycle of punishment.

Another story told by our Guru/Guide is about King Ajay. One day the king was standing in his stables supervising the care of his horses. A sadhu came and requested for alms saying that he wishes to perform some puja for which he requires money.

The king was irritated due to some problems so he said that at that moment he could give feces of the horses only. The sadhu said, "Fine then please give me that." The king gave him some feces, which the sadhu took. Later one day when the king went out on a hunting trip, he found a heap of feces of horses behind a hut. He went inside the hut to enquire. There the same sadhu was sitting and meditating. The sadhu told him that the alms given by the king have now grown into a heap because whatever one gives as alms multiplies as gains. The king got worried and asked for pardon and asked the sadhu to suggest a solution. The sadhu said that it has to be eaten by the king unless the king causes people to criticize him, which could make the feces disappear. Accepting the advice of the sadhu, the king with his daughter took a tour of his kingdom riding an elephant with colored water pretending to be consuming alcohol and flirting around. All criticized him accept one person (Saint Kabir). Accordingly the feces of the horse were reduced to a very small quantity but did not disappear completely. On enquiring, the sadhu told him that Saint Kabir had not criticized the king; therefore, small quantity of the feces is left. He requested Saint Kabir to criticize him but He refused. Then the king burnt the feces and consumed slowly. It is said that after that the sadhus started giving ashes as *vibhuti*. Moral of the story is that NEVER criticize any one. Those who are criticized gain a lot while the person who does that suffers.

Criticism in any form is bad therefore the habit of criticizing others should be dispensed with. Praise God and criticize only self. A third person should not come in between. Criticizing a Saint has dire consequences. In this connection, an incident related to Bhagat Trilochan Ji is relevant. BhagatJi's wife was fed up doing household chores and longed to have domestic help.

One day a boy came over and said that he is orphan needing help. She readily agreed to employ him. However, he said that he did not desire any salary only food, clothes and other necessities of life, but if he were criticized then he would go away. She was happy with him except for one of his habits. He ate what ever was given to him without ever asking for food even if it was not given to him at any time. If she gave ten Roti, he would eat them. She resisted asking him for some time but one day she went to a neighbor's house and shared her concern with the neighbor's wife. When she came back the servant was gone! Bhagat Ji on returning home explained to her that God Himself had come to their help but because of criticism he has gone.

Eating and Sleeping

Normally all religions permit rich as well as non- vegetarian food. Even Hinduism permits all types of food for all casts who have strenuous physical work or have to fight. However, for Brahmins there are restrictions because they are suppose to perform prayers and meditate. Sikh religion permits non-vegetarian meal provided the animal is killed in one stroke (Jhatka) but not halal, which is forbidden. However, here we are referring to those who want to meditate and attain salvation and other virtues, which go with meditation. Therefore, they have to restrict their diet to the one which would help them to attain their goals The food can be divided into three categories: -

1. **Tamsic Meal**. This is the meal which gives rise to desires and *vasna*. If one is interested in vital health and spiritual growth it is best to avoid these foods. Tamasic items include **meat**, alcohol, tobacco, onions, **garlic**, fermented foods, such as

vinegar, and stale left over food, contaminated or overripe substances. Overeating is also regarded as *tamasic*.
2. **Rajsic meal.** This is what the kings and nobles eat. It would also give rise to desires but to a lesser degree. Rajasic foods are those that have a stimulating effect on the mind and body. They are considered to be neither beneficial nor harmful. These foods lead to aggressiveness and irritability, and are often obtained in a way that harms another organism. Examples include: caffeinated drinks (such as coffee, tea (both black and green), cola drinks, and energy drinks), brown or black chocolate, paan, ginkgo biloba, overly spicy food, salty food, and the unfertilized egg.

Sattvic meal. This refers to simple meal to keep the body healthy. Non-vegetarian meals would not fall in this category. This type of meal is recommended for the meditator. Especially dinner should be light so that early morning time is fully utilized. Sattvic foods are those that lead to clarity of mind and physical health. These foods are to be consumed on a regular basis. Sattvic foods are generally those which can be obtained without harming either another organism or one's self. Only Sattvic foods are acceptable as offerings to the Hindu gods, with rare exceptions. Examples include: water, cereal grains, legumes, vegetables, fruits, nuts, unpasteurized and homogenized fresh milk and all fresh milk derivatives (mostly ghee, but also butter, cream, fresh or cottage cheese (paneer), and yogurt (lassi)), and raw honey.

Eggs are a very complicated case and don't have a clear-cut answer. Since there's debate as to the validity of the sources that categorize it as Tamasic or Rajasic, only moral insight can be provided. In olden days, eggs laid by hen could be hatched to produce chicken. But now there are so called vegetarian eggs. It is recommended that children be given such eggs as a source of calcium and proteins. In initial stages one should not worry if a cookie or biscuit or cake has egg content though eating eggs as such should be avoided. **Later on as one makes progress, even these should be avoided.**

Best food is the one**, which is cooked by the spouse or a family member because that is cooked with love and affection.** While it is being cooked, the stare from the eyes matters. Food cooked outside by commercial cooks would depend upon the mood of the cook, which can cause negative feeling. Till one starts meditating one cannot realize the vibrations coming from the food intake. Also most restaurants have vegetarian as well as non-vegetarian food which means utensils are common.

Control over sleep is a pre-requisite for meditation. For a beginner with healthy body, five hours sleep in parts is sufficient. Lesser we sleep deeper is the sleep. Sleep is also related to worries we have. A meditator who has left everything to God has no worries except that he has to please God and meditate. We have to balance our requirements with daily chores, which have to be performed since most people have to work, study or discharge other duties. Some have to work during night shift. They should find their own timings. For normal working person, about three hours sleep say from 11 PM to 02 Am is good time. From 02 to 06 AM maybe utilized for meditation, prayer and so on. From 06 to 07 Am or so one hour sleep freshens a person helping him to proceed for his daily routine work. Those who have time after lunch may again utilize an hour or so for siesta. Those who work through the day may sleep from 06 to 08 AM thus remaining fresh. Slowly one can get used to his routine in such a way that there is plenty of time for meditation. As the progress is made, one has naam repeated in one's heart through out the day and night. Further progress makes meditation itself so relaxing that requirement of sleep goes down. Amrit vela or Braham mahurat begins three hours before sunrise and continues till sunrise. Most guides normally recommend this time. However, God also has two types of courts Dewane-am (general open) and Dewane-Khas (Reserved; sort of inner cabinet). In India at Amritvela most Gurudwaras and temples become active with loud speakers beaming at full volume. This would be considered as open court. For those who want to achieve higher goals would have strive harder to join the inner cabinet. It would imply meditating between two to four AM.

LUCK AND FAITH

Let us first examine Luck Factor. Many people especially who do not have faith in God believe they are masters of their destiny and so they alone can shape their destiny. Yes one must depend on oneself for decisions; but is there nothing known as luck? Those who answer in negative, we may like to ask them do they believe in Mathematics of chance and probability? If there are two balls one red and second white in a bag, what are the chances that we will draw out a white ball? A simple 12th grade pass will answer that chances are 50 %. If there is no luck factor then from where this figure of Fifty Percent has come? In olden days if our Saints would have tried to explain mathematics, people would have called them mad but today **we know that it is true. So they called it Bhagya or destiny, which actually operates in such situations.** A decision is taken in the present and effects future, which no one has seen. So hundred percent success rates are not possible. Now this brings a question to your mind, "What should one do"? Plan properly, plan for contingencies and leave the results to God if one believes in Him or to probability theory if one feels God is redundant. However, for decisions one should take advice all right from others but decide finally oneself.

How does **luck relate to Karma theory**? We know that the path chalked out by Almighty for us is based on our deeds. Therefore, luck plays its part as per the broader design of how our life is shaped up by Him. Thus the belief that what ever has to happen will happen in spite of our efforts. On closer look one finds that a lot is in **one's own hands**. One can shape one's karma by service and recitation of naam. When karma is changed then luck would automatically change. This is where the true guide comes in. He can see both the future and past. Also after prescribing service and/or recitation, he can recommend to the Guru or the Lord for pardon which if granted can change the destiny. Thus destiny is in one's own hands but not the way non-believers say that individual should work and get results. One should carry on with what ever is required to put in the required effort but leave the results to God. At the same time seek pardon in the way prescribed above to shape one's karma to reduce dependency on luck.

SGGS says that those who meditate on His name and do service, Dharamraj (who maintains record of karma) tears their papers means all sins are pardoned if God is happy. Thus destiny is in one's own hand if one pleases God.

⤫ ⤫ ⤫

CHAPTER SEVEN

IMPORTANCE OF FORTY DAYS AND YEARS

❧❀❧

Almost all religions have something to do with this magic figure of forty days. Islam propagates fast for forty days during the holy month of Ramzan. Hinduism also recommends fast for forty days in some circumstances. There are some occasions when pundits recommend recitation of mantras for forty days. To save the trouble of reciting to the jajman (the person who is hosting the worship) they take it on themselves to do the recitation.

Even as per Christian and Hebrew beliefs number forty is important. Some of the important events associated with forty days or years are: -

1. Noah's faith was tested for forty days and nights.
2. Noah prepared the arc for 120 years a multiple of 40.
3. Saul reigned for 40 years.
4. David ruled for 40 years.
5. Solomon ruled for 40 years.
6. Lord Jesus was tested for 40 days and nights. He spends those days in wilderness till he gained victory over Satan.
7. Moses went the Mt Sinai twice to receive sermons.
8. Moses' life is divided into three parts of 40 years each.

9. Easter time for preparation with its symbolic forty days (not counting Sundays) is a high moment in Christian calendar.

As far as Sikhs are concerned, Anand Sahib has forty pauries (stanzas). Japji Sahib also has forty when Mul-Mantra and the end slok are added. In Sikhism there is a form of meditation known as Chalisa. It basically implies recitation of a stanza (Sabad) from SGGS 125K times in forty days. During this time one should refrain from any activity, which distracts one from the recitation. Food should be simple.

To complete the recitation, one has to recite the sabad 3125 times daily, which implies 29 mala of 108 beads. Bead count of 108 is counted as 100 to cater for errors. Similarly repeating the sabad caters for errors, therefore, the count works out to One Lakh (100K). Roughly it means daily 16 hours daily leaving very little time for other activities. During this period there is no restriction on diet or sleep but one should refrain from watching TV or going out unless absolutely necessary. A break can have adverse effects, therefore, should be avoided. How often one can perform chalisa depends upon the type of work which one does. Farmers and retired persons or housewives can easily carry out this activity once a year.

The sabad chosen is prefixed with mul-mantra up to nanak Hai bhi hosi such. Suffix with Satnam, Vaheguru. To sit on the bed induces sleep; therefore it should be done in a quite place.

Many people may question as to which scripture mentions that we should do chalisa. For them there can be no answers. Those who have performed chalisa can only tell what they have gained.

It is very difficult for the people who are working to perform this activity. Perhaps after retirement by those who are working chalisa can be performed. Those who are agriculturist can do it in younger ages. Because of many testing moments, which come in the way, many difficulties can be faced while doing Chalisa. Situations will be there which may be forcing a person to abandon this activity but one has to continue relentlessly.

❦ ❦ ❦

CHAPTER EIGHT

ACHEIVEMENTS

Now the question arises if we meditate would do we achieve? To understand this first we may like to look at what is the power of God. We know that it is unlimited but it also unique in many ways. AS per SGGS God is Pura (full). From this power if full is removed then again full is left. The power can be concentrated at any point and/or simultaneously spread all over the universe. When He comes to a planet in the sargun roop(primordial), he comes with requisite powers measured in *kalas*. Some of us have seen so many miracles in the present age that the achievements or powers, which are mentioned here appear to be nothing. The achievements can also be unlimited with ultimate goal being to unite with God, thus become part of that infinite entity.

When we say that **miracles** are prohibited in Sikhism, it relates to self gains or to prove oneself. The Gurus did not show any miracles when they wanted to demonstrate ways to combat the people who wanted to harm them or try to change their religion. They blessed so many people in miraculous ways. They came to the aid of the devotees when required. Only some examples have been mentioned in this narrative because they are so many miracles. Even Ram Rai Ji was sent to Aurangzeb's court armed with 72 Kalas. True Saints also have many miracles to their credit. They know whom to bless and whom to refuse.

Gains from meditation have now been **proved scientifically**. Here are some extracts from an article "Inside the Artist head" written by Kelly row published in the magazine "The Future of Everything", a Wall Street journal publication. This article helps to understand how creative a person can be if he meditates

"When Lia Chavez, a Dancer, meditates, she sees flashing lights that inspire her art. Today her visions are helping neuroscientists to understand what creativity looks like in the brain." "We got our paradigm shift when we met Lia," says Dr. Bhattachrya, who is head of the brain and cognition cluster of the psychology department at Goldsmiths, University of London, "because she happens to get inspired when she meditates, she can trigger it systematically, so long as we can give her time to get settled."

When Lia reaches a state of deep, sustained meditation, she sees strobe-like bursts of light arcing across her mind's eye, a phenomenon frequently reported by meditators. These flickers, she says are the source of her creativity and her art, and she can conjure them on command in her all white home or a more clinical setting.

"It sounds so unscientific to meditate in a lab," Chavez says. "But that's the forefront of science- to try new things."

For the past two years, she has been subjected to a battery of brain scanning experiments, meditating for eight hours at a stretch with her head covered by a wiry, swim-cap-like electroencephalograph, or EEG, monitor that tracks her brain activity. During these sessions her reports of light storms correlated with sharp increases in her neural activity, specifically her gamma waves – electromagnetic frequencies in the brain associated with aiding memory, focus and feelings of well being. But what surprised researches were where in the brain this activity was taking place. Chavez's Occipital quadrant, which processes visual stimuli, was highly active during these light filled sessions even though the artist was meditating with her eyes closed. "What she is see is not an illusion or her imagination," She says Caroline Di Bernadiluft, Bhattachariya's co-lead researcher, who lectures at Queen marry University of London. "It is coming from a primal area of her brain". When Chavez tried meditating while suffering from cold or jet lag, she saw nothing and neither did the researchers watching for spikes in her neural activity. When the artist meditated, Luft found that gamma waves activity in her occipital Quadrant pulsed at rate up to 700% higher than when she was resting.

Those who have experienced **the powers can only narrate** what can be gained. Even that to be expressed is difficult as mentioned in SGGS that if one asks a dumb fellow the taste of sweats he has eaten he cannot say anything. Still an attempt is made to describe few gains possible.

First of all He entices a person with **wealth**. The wealth received can be so much that we may get tired of receiving it. Those who fall pray to it get entangled in wealth and remains so. SGGS says, "if we meditate for wealth, which is obtained only through previous karmas then the meditation is wasted". He gives sufficient to a person who is truly devoted so that he may not run into difficulties but not more to safeguard against greed, which can set in.

A person who meditates regularly seldom dies accidentally. Almighty protects him. Sometimes God sends good souls (shahid) to provide him protection. Some devotees were traveling to Delhi from Meerut in a car at night. En-route they fell asleep. Next they knew was when they reached their destination that is the place where their Guru was. Of course the Guru who said that He had to summon Shahid Souls to drive them to their destination and scolded them. Sahid souls are the souls, which have not yet taken next birth for variety of reasons and are waiting for the right time and parents. They also come to places where there is Kirtan and prayers are being recited. Bad souls congregate near bars and other such places.

Second power is to rule over others. Leaders are born because they have lot of credit of meditation and prayers but what they do decides their future. Many kings have perished because of their misdeeds. They may then get next birth in low caste or in the animal form. Those leaders, who are virtuous and further the cause of God, continue getting good bodies in their next birth.

Third power is described by those who have seen with their own eyes describe the miracles, which can take place. They have seen people blind from birth regaining their eye sight, deaf being able to hear, cancer patients in the last stages getting cured, even those declared dead have been able to live for a long time. This all can happen provided the guide or the Guru is karniyuog (realized souls)

Fourth power is obtained through **religious practices**. This is not very well known to common persons specially in the West, though Muslim Pirs and Christian Saints are known to posses such powers associated with miracles. As per Eastern thought there are eighteen powers like seeing happenings anywhere in the universe (dib drishti) or hearing anything said anywhere, reading others mind, traveling at the speed of mind which is the only practical method of travel in the universe. Many people tend to dispose off dib drishti and other powers described in Mahabharata and other scriptures as science fiction. They have never meditated nor are aware of what exactly these powers are.

Following are some Supernatural Powers:

Ridhi-Sidhi

These are supernatural powers, and include Ridhi, Sidhi, Nau-Nidhi, Budhi, and Mukti -

Ridhi

It is attainment, success, progress, and affluence. Literally, Ridhi also means cooked-food. The practitioner of the Naam becomes widely known (influential), and the people start bringing him or her all sorts of foods, eatables, gifts, and other commodities - one of his attainments.

Sidhi

Occult, i.e. supernatural powers. One can be present at more than one places at one and the same time, can make prophesies, become invisible, get power to fly, can make things happen, bless (and curse) others, produce things from nowhere, bring back life to the dead, and solve problems of the others. His or her Hamzad (astral-self) can separate from the gross body and visit places etc. Such powers come naturally as well. Power to change ones body with another when on verge of death, can be developed. Some may get the power to die at will, and even of automatic self-immolation of his or her dead body. The practitioner (meditator) does not usually long or works for them. He is not supposed to display his or her prowess. Moreover, these are considered to be of no great merit, as they are considered to be interference in the Lord's plans, and are a hindrance in the God realization. These do not lead to emancipation. Supernatural powers are attachments; these do not permit the Naam to get set in the mind). 5-593-18

Sidhis are 18. (Shabdarath, S,G,P.C., 1986, Page 10).

Minor Sidhis

These are ten:

- Door-Darshan - to see all, clairvoyance.
- Door-Sarvan - to hear all, clairaudience.
- Par-Kaya Parvesh - ability to enter other's body. To rejuvenate, he may discard his own old body and enter that of a (dying) young person.
- Annuram - freedom from hunger and thirst.
- Kaamroop - adopt desired form, ability to change the form to that of another person.
- Savichhatt-Mirtu - to die at will, to die the way one wants to.
- Sankalap Sidhi - to get desires fulfilled, to have all that one wants.
- Apprittehatt-Gatee - ability to go anywhere without any hindrance or obstruction.

- Mano-Veg - to go anywhere at the speed of thought.
- Sur-Kareer.a - to have enjoyment along with gods, to join them in enjoyments (merry making).

Major Sidhis

These are eight:

- Anima - ability to become very small, minute.
- Mahema - to become big, gain colossal size.
- Garima - to become heavy, gain an excessive weight.
- Laghima - to become light, subtle.
- Praptee - to get success, achieve goals, and get fulfilled.
- Prakamya - to read the minds of other people.
- Eeshihta (Isatva) - lordliness, and power to persuade others.
- Vashihta (Vasitva) - to control other's mind. Self control - control over all senses.

Nau-Nidhi

Nidhis are nine types of treasures - (Page 506, Gur Shabad Ratnakar, Kahn Singh, Bhasha Vibhag, 1960. Shabdarath, S,G,P.C., 1986, Page 10).

- Padam-Nidhi - attainment of sons, grand sons, gold, silver, i.e. the precious metals.
- Mahan-Padam - one gets diamonds, rubies and other gems and jewels (precious stones).
- Kharab - riches of all kinds.
- Kund - trading in gold.
- Neel - trading in precious stones, jewels, and gems.
- Sankh - delicious eatables (Procuring from nowhere).

- Kachhap - clothes and food-grains in abundance, no shortage.
- Mukund - mastery in arts, music, and poetry.
- Makar - gives the art of using weapons and sovereignty on others.

Nidhis give property, products of land and sea, servants, health, wisdom, animals and conveyance etc. An adept gets accepted, respected, and honored by everyone. The people start giving him each and everything imaginable.

Budhi

Wisdom. He becomes a Brahm-Giani: one with the knowledge about God - a **realized person**. Defined in the Eighth Ashtpadi of Sukhmani Sahib (part of Sri Guru Granth Sahib). This confirms the practitioner into -

- Bharosa - **faith**. A deep faith and dependence on God. A firm faith in Waheguru (God) is the first and the foremost experience of the practitioner of the Naam-Jaap. He becomes a firm believer that God is one and there is none other like Him, He is the Creator, Doer, everywhere, Omnipotent and everything is under His will.
- Leenta - an absolute attachment (absorption) to God.
- Santokh - contentment (on destiny).
- Detachment - from the dear ones and the worldly possessions.
- Hukam - acceptance of the will of God. It is total surrender to Him.
- Sehaj - equilibrium, equi-poise.
- Anand - perpetual delight, permanent joy.
- Vismaad - ecstasy: Joy plus wonderment, forgetting the self.

- Nidar - benevolence of God. He believes in the mercy of God as an instrument of his attainments, and that his own efforts mean nothing. This attitude keeps him free from ego. His efforts are needed to make him fit for the mercy of God.

Up to here these powers refer to this world, hence can be misused if wrong people get them. These powers are not obtained in one birth. It takes a long time.

A meditator should **reject** these as they are thrown in the path to wean him away. Once he clears the tests, these powers follow him, which enables him to guide others by seeing what they are doing or what they are thinking or what is their past and future.

Mukti or Moksh (Salvation)

This power refers to liberation from the worldly attachments, transmigration, and from the cycle of birth and death (reincarnation). These are the characteristics of a Mukat (emancipated, liberated person). In the first stage of Mukti, the record of deeds is taken over by the Guru from Dharamraj (the god of death)

Char-Padarath

Four boons are - Dharam, Arath, Kaam, and Moksh. These four are the usual goals of life for everyone - an ethical discipline of life, assets to fulfill the needs, marriage and children, and in the end liberation.

- **Dharam - discipline**. Understanding of his or her duties i.e. virtues (ethics).

- **Arath - assets.** He or she has no dearth of money - precious metals, pearls, and stones. Gets all the wealth.
- **Kaam - desires.** His or her all desires get fulfilled and it covers marriage and children.
- **Moksh** - redemption (liberation). He or she attains emancipation.

Traaekaal-Drishti, Vaak-Sidhi

Traaekaal Drishti - Triple-Vision (three-dimensional), all knowing. **He can see (know) all that happened in the past, is going on now, and will come tomorrow (omniscient).** The powers of intuition and prophecy develop; he will know things before these happen, can make predictions and foretell his own end. These experiences should be taken as indicators of progress. Boasting about them creates an ego, which hinders further advancement of the practitioner. Commonly, the people think that these should be kept secret. Of course, one should share these only with the right persons. Such things motivate others to do the Naam-Jaap. The Guru advises to recite His name and to attach others to do so. **Vaak-Sidhi - Whatever he or she says comes to pass (happens). It is generally advised that anyone practicing the Naam, should never let anything unwanted escape from his or her mouth.**

Samm-Drishti, Turi-aa-Avastha

Samm-Drishti - No discrimination. Everyone is one and the same to him. He perceives God in everything and everyone. Turiyaa Avastha - Chautha-Padd (Fourth Dimension). It implies going higher then the three states of Maya (mundane, the worldly things) i.e. ego, evil and virtue. The world is a play of these three dimensions. Turiaa Avastha means the Fourth State i.e. detachment from these three characteristics of the world, and transcending them (Transcendental Meditation).

Deh Abhav (Devi Vesh)

It is referred to in Jaapji Sahib. One feels that one's body is no more. The body-sense disappears. With the Naam-Jaap, one rises to such a level of absorption in God that **one has no more to do with the body**. When there is no body sense, there is **no affliction or pain**. He or she gets detached from the physical existence, and goes **above the fear of disease and death**. There is no disease or death for such a realized person. To keep him or her alive, others have to take his or her care.

(Retrieved from http://www.sikhiwiki.org/index.php/ Supernatural_Powers)

A true guide has all the above powers and trust of God and Guru that he would use them for the good of people and to direct them towards God.

Darshan. Visions or Darshan can of many types as one progresses in meditation. First of all one feels inner voices, which are discernable. Sometimes if one has a quest for vision then the voice may disappear. It is better not to wish for visions in such situations because guiding voice is better than vision once and then blankness. Gradually when one progresses, vision comes in dreams, then by feeling. Later on further progress one sees God in the desired form with open eyes. Those who are realized souls can have darshan in human body form. In such forms there is lot of light, which is not very easy to withstand.

Person who has not reached higher stages can faint or may be unable to withstand the vision.

Those who think this is a hoax, here are two true incidents.

In the year 1944, there was a patrol send out by a battalion of Punjab Regiment, forming part of 4th Infantry Division (Indian) deployed in Italy under Subedar(equivalent of Warrant Officer) Balwant Singh. It was ambushed by Germans, which forced the leader and one more survivor to run for their life and hide in a cave. In two days they exhausted their emergency ration and water. Then Subedar Balwant remembered that he had attended sermons of his guide a great saint of Punjab. He took out his boots and prayed to the Babaji. After one and half hour they heard a lady's voice saying, " I know that you two are in the cave; I have brought food for you". They came out and saw an old lady. She gave them food and water and took them to her home. En-route she narrated that she is a devotee of Lord Christ for past at least forty years. But on that day a miracle occurred (at the time when Balwant Singh was praying). Lord Christ gave her darshan (vision) and told her about these two soldiers and instructed her to give food and water, then take them home and further guide them to their defense lines. The figure of Lord Christ kept changing into someone with a turban and Lord Christ. She left them at their defense lines. This episode was mentioned in the Divisional Liaison letter stating how an English Fairy led these two soldiers to safety. Subedar Balwant on return to India narrated it to Brig Partap Singh Jaspal (Retd) who has mentioned it in his book as well as in the video.

Second Incident occurred in 1943. A Muslim Police inspector was posted in Hoshiarpur (Punjab-India). He was a devotee of a Muslim **Pir (Muslim Saint)**. The Honorable Pir told him to go to Ludhiana a nearby place and have darshan of a sikh saint who was the supreme pir at that moment and would leave the world shortly. When he went there, he sat down in the last row attending the sermons. At the end of the sermons, Babaji whom he had never met earlier called him by name and said why has your honorable Pir send you to me? He is capable of granting any boon to you. **These two incidents also prove that there is only one God though the religions are different. There is nothing to fight over this issue or trying to convert people from one religion to another because of sense of righteousness.**

There is an old lady who lost her husband recently. Initially she was overcome by feeling of loneliness but soon with some guidance she started reading and listening to religious books. This gave her insight into the concept of meditation, which she started practicing. Soon she has reached a stage where continuously naam is being recited in her mind 24 × 7. Thus instead of spending her remaining years in grieve after the death of her spouse she has made full use of the time and reached much higher stages of meditation.

A Sikh clergyman went to UK where he was taken to a person of European origin. He was surprised when that person told him to remove his shoes and cover his head as if he was entering a holy place. On entering he was surprised to see a beautiful photo of the Golden temple (Harminder Sahib). On enquiring the Englishman narrated his story. He had gone on an organized tour of Pakistan and India. When they reached Lahore, a Muslim person gave him some coins and requested him to offer them at the Golden Temple on his behalf, since they were going to Amritsar. The English man asked him that being a Muslim how is it that he believes in Golden Temple. He replied that the Headquarters of all religions is the Golden Temple. He also advised the Englishman that when he goes there he must go with full faith and follow the method prescribed for the visit. This way he would be able to reap all benefits. Following his advice, the Englishman went to Golden temple wearing a turban with full faith. There he had visions, which made him stay there for many days. He told his touring partners that they could go to Agra and other places but he would stay in Amritsar. On their return, they could pick him up for the journey back to UK. Narrating above incident, the Englishman said that after the visit he could hear live kirtan from Harminder Sahib with his ears (Dur-Sarvana) without using any device.

Another incident relates to power of reciting Japji Sahib. A Saint (Hindu) had his ashram near Agra. Access to his ashram was through a village only because between his ashram and the highway was land belonging to a Sikh gentleman. While constructing the Ashram, the saint thought that the Sikh gentleman would give him access, as only about 12 feet track was required. However, the Sikh gentleman was adamant that he would not part with a single inch of his land. The saint tried all methods including action by coercion but of no avail. He then gave a thought and decided to invoke blessings of Guru Gobind Singhji. He took bath, sat in a clean place and recited Japji Sahib with full concentration. After that he conveyed his request to the Guru. Next day morning the Sikh gentleman came and asked the Saint to take the required access in the form of a track. The saint asked him as to what made him change his mind. The Sikh gentleman told him that at night in dream Guru Gobind Singhji scolded him and told him that the saint is a pious man so the access must be provided. That day onwards the saint goes to Patna Sahib, the Birth Place of Guru Gobind Singhji, every year.

Tantric Powers

These powers are referred to powers obtained through meditation by some people who misuse these for personal gains. They also entice people to come to them since they can do black magic and harm their enemies. A person who wishes to meditate and gain ultimate goals should NEVER go to such persons or seek *Tavits* (metal piece with mantras chanted to make it powerful) or threads and so on, which can cause harm to others. God seldom pardons such people.

❧ ❧ ❧

CHAPTER NINE

SUMMARY

⸙

To conclude therefore, we could summarize all the recommendations as given below.

- Meditation is common to all religions. It is the best way to achieve salvation and other worldly objectives.
- There is no need to leave the house and go to a forest or away from the family.
- To begin with one should take out about 2.5 hours for meditation and prayers.
- Early morning (Amrit vela or Braham murth) is best time as it very peaceful time. Depending upon nature of work one should find suitable time.
- Prayers and meditation must be done Nishkam (without any demands).
- Guru and a guide in human form would help immensely and accelerate the process of achieving objectives. Obeying all their commands one must perform Service of the Guru and guide.
- One should get out of bed; select a quite place in the house for meditation. Ideal is to have a room earmarked for SGGS or prayers.
- Recite naam. For Sikhs mul-mantra till Nanak hosi bhi sach or Vaheguru or any other prescribed by the guide is recommended. For Hindus word Ram or Gobind or the

word given by the guide is ideal. Similarly for followers of Islam, Rahim is recommended. Christians generally recite a stanza from the Bible.

- The concentration should be on the lotus feet of the Guru or blankness as one is comfortable with.
- Service of the deity or SGGS and service of community forms part of meditation. May it be in Gurudwaras, Community meals, Temples or other places like Ashrams. Ashrams like Mother Teresa's Ashram are very pious where there is no corruption.
- Ten percent of the income (post tax) should be earmarked for charity. Best is to have a separate bank account for that purpose because opportunity for donation does not present itself at all times. If mixed up with normal check in account then there is a tendency to use it for normal expenditure. Sponsoring of a child for education, donation to ashrams, *langar* (the community kitchen) building of religious places and so on are some of the things which qualify for charity.
- Start meditating without waiting for obtaining purity of mind but gradually work towards it.
- Develop the habit of speaking softly. Speak only *Amritvani* (life giving words).
- Neither criticize any body, nor hear criticism of anybody.
- Have only one spouse and never get involved in adultery.
- Stick to satvic food consisting of vegetarian meals only.
- Earn legitimate money without getting involved in mal practices or accepting graft. Refrain from greed.
- Perform all duties towards family but keep in mind that all are responsible for their karma. Remain detached from all.
- Have **faith** in almighty, Guru and the guide. The best path is the one chalked out by Him for you. Do not try to change the path by prayers.

- Get rid of jealousy, hatred and anger, as they are the biggest killers.
- Remember ego is the greatest enemy, which can bring one down to start point or even below.
- Develop compassion and humility.
- NEVER visit a tantric.
- See God in all beings.
- Do not get involved in arguments or discussion with a non-believer. It is not only waste of time but also it can lead to criticism, which can be fetal.
- Do not get side tracked by the tests and obstacles thrown by Almighty in your path in the form of wealth, power and spiritual powers.
- Align your self to God- Guru- guide, seeing and feeling God in all of them.
- Darshan (visions) may be in the form of voice, feeling, in the form of Guru or Deity or simple light. It will not be easy to bear it. Do not be afraid. Those who have experienced it narrate that when power comes it is not easy to absorb.
- In the final stages one may experience vision of all primordial of our world and those of the entire universe. All those who have appeared so far and those who will appear in future till next parlay (end of the universe).

❦ ❦ ❦

CONCLUSIONS

❦

Through this book, an attempt has been made to bring forward a practical prospective of meditation and love for God. Practical methods have been suggested without getting in to too much technical jargon or getting involved in what the scriptures say. The Part One is a reference point for what is generally understood by meditation, prayers and other methods of pleasing God. Part two is based on experiences direct and indirect, meaning what has been gathered by interacting with various realized persons.

It is hoped that those who read this book would follow the righteous path and achieve their objectives. During past ages like satyug and others achieving these objectives was not easy since most people were pious and devoted. Therefore to stand out one had meditate for many years or perhaps for many births. During present age where sins, greed and desires have increased to uncontrolled proportions, salvation is easier and obtainable in shorter time. The saying "Andon men kana raja" (among blind people one eyed person is the king) is valid. Therefore, we must make hay when the sun shines, as Satyug is about to return.

❦ ❦ ❦

ABOUT THE AUTHOR

The author, a retired army officer, had served in the army for thirty-five years. He earned his PhD (stress management) just before retirement. After retirement he had been teaching management students for six years. During all these years he has interacted with various realized persons. Gains from all the experiences have been shared in this book.

He has following publications to his credit:-

- Stress Management: integrated Eastern and Western Approach.
- Motivation: Theory of Prerna. (Co-author)
- Significance of customer relationship in enhancing customer equity. (Co-author).

He can be reached at

grewaljagtar13@gmail.com
Telephone : +13027404164
+91-9872821730

www.ingramcontent.com/pod-product-compliance
Lightning Source LLC
Chambersburg PA
CBHW020509040426
42331CB00042BA/101

GFIOM Publications @ 2019

Copyright © 2019 GFIOM
P.O. Box KF1943
Koforidua, Eastern Region, Ghana

Email: tfogiom@rocketmail.com

Scriptures are taken from the King James Version (KJV). KING JAMES VERSION, public domain

Entire contents otherwise Copyright @2019 by Frederick Amon-Armah
Published by GFIOM in cooperation with
QUEST PUBLICATIONS, Ontario, Canada.

Published in Canada.
Printed in the United States of America

Cover Design by Quest Publications.
Interior Formatting & Layout by Quest Publications
(questpublications@outlook.com)

ISBN-13: 978-1-988439-21-1

CONTENTS

Foreword .... *viii*

Introduction ....*x*

THE THREE "Rs" OF THE BLOOD OF JESUS 1

   REDEMPTION 1

   REGENERATION...7

   RESTORATION...9

WHY THE BLOOD IN PRAYER?........................... 11

33 DAYS OF PRAYER 14

   DAY 1 14

   DAY 2 14

   DAY 3 15

   DAY 4 16

   DAY 5 17

   DAY 6 18

   DAY 7 19

   DAY 8 20

   DAY 9 21

   DAY 10 22

   DAY 11 23

   DAY 12 23

   DAY 13 24

   DAY 14 25

DAY 15 25

DAY 16 26

DAY 17 27

DAY 18 28

DAY 19 29

DAY 20 30

DAY 21 31

DAY 22 31

DAY 23 32

DAY 24 33

DAY 25 34

DAY 26 35

DAY 27 35

DAY 28 36

DAY 29 37

DAY 30 38

DAY 31 39

DAY 32 39

DAY 33 40

ABOUT THE BOOK.. 43

ABOUT THE AUTHOR 44

FOREWORD

by Godwin Kofi Ahlijah Ph.D.

33 DAYS OF PRAYING THROUGH THE BLOOD OF JESUS is not only a prayer book but gives an exegetical insight into what the simple but often confused concept of salvation is all about.

Variant views on salvation are among the main fault lines dividing the various Christian denominations, impeding the spread of the gospel in many areas of the world. Not to mention believers who have accepted the Lord Jesus as their Saviour, and yet walk in fear and anxiety, because of their fundamental lack of understanding of the power in appropriating the blood of Jesus.

The author, Evangelist Fredrick Amon-Armah, carefully explains the three stages of salvation in a scholarly, but yet simple steps. He establishes the importance of understanding the total salvation package and the need to profess daily the dominion believers have over sin and its consequences.

Evangelist Fredrick could best be described as a "praying General". He is one who walks the talk. This book is a result of his personal victory over the shackles of the enemy by praying daily through the efficacy of the blood of Jesus.

This masterpiece is a must read for all who seek to be victorious in their walk with the Lord and could be a great bible study tool for pastors and church leaders. We all wait in anticipation for the second volume and subsequent revelations from the bosom of this resourceful intellectual "prayer General".

Enjoy your journey through this book.

> **And they overcame him by the BLOOD OF THE LAMB and by the word of their testimony; and they loved not their lives unto death.**
>
> —*Revelation 12:11 (NKJV)*

INTRODUCTION

... that if you confess with your mouth the Lord Jesus and believe in your heart that God has raised Him from the dead, you will be saved. For with the heart one believes unto righteousness, and with the mouth confession is made unto salvation.

—*Romans 10:9-10 (NKJV)*

The word of God as inspired by the Holy Spirit and written through his sent ones, the Apostles and Prophets is not only for us to believe. As a matter of fact, believing is just one step but does not complete the process of salvation. The book of James expounds the fact that believing is not the end.

You believe that there is one God. You do well. Even the demons believe--and tremble! But do you want to know, O foolish man, that faith without works is dead?

—*James 2:19-20 (NKJV)*

James 2:19-20 exposes the fact that believing alone does not get you saved. Demons believe God but they cannot be saved. James hinges on actions, thus obeying and doing what the scriptures have said is a proof of your belief and that endorses your salvation, which demons cannot do. They are only limited to believing.

In Romans 10:9 the emphasis is on the message of faith that is being preached to sinners. The writer declares that if one confesses with his/her mouth the Lord Jesus and believes in his/her heart that God has raised Him from the dead, s/he shall be saved. This connotes that without these two conditions; of believing and confessing (which signifies action to the belief), salvation is not complete. In the verse 10, he now declares that believing in your heart can make one righteous or give one a right standing with God but until one confesses, s/he has not affirmed his or her salvation. Confessing the word of God is an act of affirming, endorsing and enforcing ones belief which brings the belief from its abstract or provisional state into a real and definite state. Our confession is in three folds: (1) Practicing the word of God through faith, (2) Confessions by faith, (3) Enforcing the word through prayer by faith.

In the same way, after confessing Jesus Christ as our Lord unto salvation, that is not the end. Our salvation is in three folds; the salvation or regeneration of our spirits, the salvation of our souls and finally the salvation of our bodies which is our transformation from mortality into immortality with glorious bodies. The first phase of our salvation involves the forgiveness of our sins, the washing or cleansing away of our sins by the blood of Jesus which gives us access to God. According to Ephesians 2:1-9:

> *We are made alive, who were dead in trespasses and sins, in which we once walked according to the course of this world, according to the prince of the power of the air, the spirit who now works in the sons of disobedience, among whom also we all once conducted ourselves in the lusts of our flesh, fulfilling the desires of the flesh and of the mind, and were by nature children of wrath, just as the others. But God, who is rich in mercy, because of His great love with which He loved us, even when we were dead in trespasses, made us alive together with Christ (by grace you have been saved), and raised us up together, and made us sit together in the heavenly places in Christ Jesus, that in the*

ages to come He might show the exceeding riches of His grace in His kindness toward us in Christ Jesus. For by grace you have been saved through faith, and that not of yourselves; it is the gift of God, not of works, lest anyone should boast.

Thus, concerning the first phase of our salvation, we (our spirit man) were dead, alienated from God who is Spirit and the source of life for our spirits. However, as we believe and confess Jesus Christ as our Lord and saviour, believing that he demonstrated his love for us by dying in our place on the cross and was raised on the third day, we are given life or reconciled to God (Romans 5:10). By believing that we are sinners and confessing our sins, we are forgiven and cleansed by the washing of sins with the blood of Jesus Christ. We become born of the Spirit and hence spirit beings after our father (John 3:5-6). Therefore, we boldly go before the thrown of grace to obtain mercy and find grace to help in time of need (Hebrews 4:16).

The second phase; the salvation of our souls is a continuous process while we are still here on earth in the flesh. This comes by continually hearing the word of God; which increases our faith (Romans 10:17), by confessing, affirming and enforcing the word of God which is the application of the word. Receiving the end of our faith, the salvation of our souls (1 Peter 1:9). Therefore, we lay aside all filthiness and overflow of wickedness and receive with meekness the implanted word which is able to save our souls (James 1:21). We are able to do this because our spirit man is saved and alive (we are reconciled with God) which is the first phase or dimension of our salvation. The salvation of our souls also involve our fellowship with the Holy Spirit and nurturing of our spirits to grow in Christ so that we reflect him in our natural bodies and life here on earth. We do not draw back to perdition but we believe unto the saving of our souls (life) (Hebrews 10:39). **The second phase is the basis for which we need to pray the scriptures, not only believing but confessing with our mouths what we believe and enforcing this through prayer.** For we are God's workmanship, created in Christ Jesus for good works, which He prepared beforehand that we should walk in them (Ephesians 2:10). Nonetheless, the kingdom of God since the days of John the Baptist until now, suffers violence and the violent take it by force (Matthew 11:12). That is why the Apostle John said "I wish above all things that you may prosper and be in good health even as your soul prospers. **As much as your souls prosper, your physical life will also prosper.**

The first dimension of our salvation which is the salvation of our spirit is by the saving grace which is a free gift to all. In the second phase we build on this grace by working out our salvation (the salvation of our souls) with fear and trembling by practicing and living the word and by praying the word through supplication, petition and warfare. The word of God concerning the salvation of our souls after our spirits are regenerated as long as we are here on earth is provisional. Until we agree with it, live by it, practice it, preach it and pray it, the written word of God containing His promises and will for us remains provisional instead of definite in our lives. We need not only believe the written word of God but pray it into reality in our lives. **The reason for this book is to contribute to the second phase of our salvation (the salvation of our souls or lives here on earth). Thus, to enable the reader to enforce the finished works of our Lord Jesus Christ on the cross in our lives by presenting evidence (proof) which is the word of God that nullifies the holdings and accusations of Satan against the believer.**

The third phase or dimension of our salvation is the salvation of our bodies which is our transformation from mortality to immortality where death is swallowed in victory as noted in 1 Corinthians 15:51-54 and 1 Thessalonians 4:14-17.

> *Listen, I will tell you God's hidden purpose! We shall not all have passed to our rest, but we shall all be transformed-in a moment, in the twinkling of an eye, At the last trumpet-call; for the trumpet will sound, and the dead will rise immortal, and we, also, shall be transformed. For this perishable body of ours must put on an imperishable form, and this dying body a deathless form. And, when this dying body has put on its deathless form, then indeed will the words of Scripture come true: Death has been swallowed up in victory! Where, O Death, is thy victory? Where, O Death, is thy sting?'*
>
> —*1 Corinthians 15:51-54 (TCNT)*

> *For if we believe that Jesus died and rose again, even so God will bring with Him those who sleep in Jesus. For this we say to you by the word of the Lord, that we who are alive and remain until the coming of the Lord will by no means precede those*

who are asleep. For the Lord Himself will descend from heaven with a shout, with the voice of an archangel, and with the trumpet of God. And the dead in Christ will rise first. Then we who are alive and remain shall be caught up together with them in the clouds to meet the Lord in the air. And thus we shall always be with the Lord.

—*1 Thessalonians 4:14-17 (NKJV)*

We have been redeemed, we are being redeemed and we shall be redeemed. Thus, as we are working out our salvation, we are also waiting for the redemption of our bodies which is nearer than we first believed, having in mind that we are in the last days.

Not only that, but we also who have the first fruits of the Spirit, even we ourselves groan within ourselves, eagerly waiting for the adoption, the redemption of our body.

—*Romans 8:23 (NKJV)*

And do this, knowing the time, that now it is high time to awake out of sleep; for now, our salvation is nearer than when we first believed.

—*Romans 13:11 (NKJV)*

In Him you also trusted, after you heard the word of truth, the gospel of your salvation; in whom also, having believed, you were sealed with the Holy Spirit of promise, who is the guarantee of our inheritance UNTIL THE REDEMPTION OF THE PURCHASED POSSESSION, to the praise of His glory.

—*Ephesians 1:13-14 (NKJV)*

THE THREE "Rs"
OF THE BLOOD OF JESUS

REDEMPTION

In Him we have redemption through His blood, the forgiveness of sins, according to the riches of His grace.

—*Ephesians 1:7 (NKJV)*

According to the New International Dictionary of the Bible (1987), redemption literally means release or freedom on payment of a price, deliverance by a costly method. In my own literal translation, to redeem means to take back that which was originally yours by costly way (that is paying a price).

Then God said, "Let Us make man in Our image, according to Our likeness; LET THEM HAVE DOMINION OVER the fish of the SEA, over the birds of the AIR, and over the cattle, OVER ALL THE EARTH and over every creeping thing that creeps on the earth." So God created man in His own image; in the image of God He created him; male and female He created them. Then

God blessed them, and God said to them, "Be fruitful and multiply; fill the earth and subdue it; have dominion over the fish of the sea, over the birds of the air, and over every living thing that moves on the earth."

—*Genesis 1:26-28 (NKJV).*

In Gen 1:26-28, we see God giving authority to man. From the account of the fall of Adam, we understand that all mankind fell after the fall of the first man, Adam. For by one man sin entered into the world, and death by sin; and so death passed upon all men, for that all have sinned (Romans 5:12). For all have sinned and fall short of the glory of God (Romans 3:23). Adam's disobedience broke the covering of God over mankind and handed over authority given to him by God to the devil. Satan took over the management and governance of mankind and the world. In the gospel of Luke 4:5-7, the devil took Jesus Christ to a high mountain and showed him all the kingdoms of the world in a moment of time and said to him, "All this authority I will give to you, and their glory for this has been delivered to me, and I give it to whomever I wish. Therefore if you will worship before me, all will be yours". Indeed, the world was (is) under the government of Satan because man had lost the authority, glory, covering and nature of God.

God in his rich grace and mercy sought to redeem mankind which he could have done so easily but being a just God, he had bound himself with his word that without the shedding of blood there is no remission of sins (Hebrew 9:22). He hated sin but had to deal with sin so he could get the sinner (mankind) back to himself. Though he had instituted the sacrifices of bulls and goats for the forgiveness of sins, these could not wash away or cleanse the sins of mankind because the blood of animals were inferior (Hebrews 9:12-14; 10:4-8). He had to shed a superior blood without blemish and spot to cleanse the sins of mankind.

In Leviticus 16:1-34, scriptures talk about the 'Day of Atonement' which was a day when the sins of Israel were covered for one year. In Hebrew, the Day of Atonement is known as *Yom Kippur*. Yom means "the day" and Kippur means "to cover." This means that sins were not washed or cleansed but was only covered by the blood of animals. On this day, the High Priest offers a sacrifice for his own sins and for the sins of Israel. He offers a bull for his own sin offering to make atonement for himself and his household. Then he

3

offers a goat as sin offering for the people of Israel. Each year, he would select two young male goats which he presented to the Lord. He would cast lots to determine which one of the goats would be "the Lord's goat" to be killed, and which one would become "the scapegoat" to be set free (Leviticus 16:7-10). The High Priest would then tie a scarlet rope made of wool around the neck of the Lord's goat and another scarlet rope around the horns of the scapegoat. The Lord's goat was then slaughtered and its blood taken into the Holy of Holies in the Temple and sprinkled on the mercy seat, which was the lid of the Ark of the Covenant (Leviticus 16:15-20). The High Priest would then lay his hands on the head of the scapegoat and confess the sins of the people. Afterwards, the scapegoat was led out by a designated person of the temple and into the wilderness where it was released (Leviticus 16:21-22).

While "the Lord's goat" was killed as a sacrifice for sins, the "scapegoat" was set free. This is the same scenario that Pontius Pilate demonstrated when he presented two men. A scarlet rope was put on the Lord's goat. A scarlet robe was put on Jesus (Matt. 27:28).

It was the custom to release one prisoner at the Passover. Barabbas was guilty of murder and sentenced to die for his crimes (Mark 15:7) but Jesus had done nothing. He was accused of being the King of the Jews. In fact, he accepted the accusation of being King of the Jews, so that we can become Kings and Priests in His Kingdom being washed by his blood.

Then Pilate asked Him, saying, "Are You the King of the Jews?" He answered him and said, "It is as you say" So Pilate said to the chief priests and the crowd, "I find no fault in this Man." Matthew 23:3-4 (NKJV)

Just like the High Priest would cast lots to determine the Lord's goat and the scapegoat, Pontius Pilate brought Jesus and Barabbas before the crowd and asked which one they wanted released. The people chose Barabbas, thus, he became the scapegoat. After the High Priest released the scapegoat he washed his hands (Ex. 30:19, Lev. 16:24). Pontius Pilate also washed his hands after he had released Barabbas (Matt. 27:24). Jesus Christ was sacrificed like the Lord's goat but this time, unlike the Day of Atonement where the High Priest sprinkled the blood, Jesus Christ himself being our Great High Priest presented his own blood in the Holy Place in Heaven before the presence of Father to redeem us eternally (Hebrews 9:12;25). He became our substitute and died in our place. Barabbas who is the scapegoat represents all of us walking away free while Jesus died in our place. The sins of Israel were covered for one year (Leviticus 16:34) but by the shedding of the blood of Jesus Christ, sin is washed away forever. God satisfied himself and his just nature by sacrificing his only begotten son for the remission of our sins once and for all. Thus, God paid a ransom by the blood of Jesus Christ to release or free us from the captivity of Sin, Satan and Self. The 'word' 'purchased' or 'paid for' does not mean God paid something to the devil to release us but by the costly manner in which God satisfied himself based on his own word according to Hebrews 9:22.

Therefore, sacrifices of goats for the remission of sin in the Old Testament as was instructed by God to the High Priest was a typology of how God wanted to present Jesus Christ to be sacrificed. The difference was that his blood was superior and could cleanse the sins of mankind once and for all from generation to generation. The blood of Jesus still flows, it is powerful and it still speaks (Hebrews 12:24) and was shed for our redemption.

REGENERATION

The Greek word for regeneration is *palingenesia, palin* means again and *genesis* means birth. Therefore, regeneration simply means new birth, a new beginning, a new order. After we have been 'purchased' or liberated from Sin, Satan and Self. We are adopted into sonship, thus to become like him. He imputes himself into us. Thus we are regenerated.

When Adam sinned, the man lost the nature of God and the life of God. The spiritual DNA of man was denatured by the virus called sin which had no remedy or cure except the blood of Jesus Christ. This virus is passed on to every man born of a woman by a natural process of sperm of a man fertilizing an egg from a woman making us sinners. This why in God's own wisdom, Jesus Christ was not born through a natural process, but by the coming upon of the Holy Spirit and the overshadowing power of God on Mary (Luke 1:35). Thus, our Lord Jesus Christ escaped the sin virus that is transmitted to anyone born on earth through the natural means which makes the DNA of God in us denatured from day one of fertilization in a mother's womb. That is why it is written in 2 Corinthians 5:21 that God made Jesus who knew no sin (who was not a sinner) to be sin for us, that we might become the righteousness of God. In other words he became sin that we can become sons for all mankind had sinned when Adam sinned (Romans 3:23; Romans 5:12; 1 Corinthians 15:21).

Regeneration can be broken down into 'Re' and 'Gene'. In biology, we understand that genes make up DNA. Consequently, due to the denaturation of the DNA resulting from the sin virus we lost our original spiritual genetic make-up thus our identity and nature. The blood of Jesus washes the sin virus away and 're-gene' us to renaturates our spiritual DNA into the original DNA of God. When God re-gene us, he reconstitutes our spiritual genetic make-up. So it is written therefore, if anyone is in Christ, he is a new creation; old things have passed away; behold, all things have become new (2 Corinthians 5:17) and unless a man be born again (re-gene) he cannot see the Kingdom of God (John 3:3). Further, it is written that God did not save us by works of righteousness which we have done, but according to His mercy, through the washing of regeneration and renewing of the Holy Spirit (Titus 3:5). By the washing of regeneration, our inherently sinful nature is changed into the Holy nature of God.

The blood of Jesus Christ is not only a ransom for our redemption but the blood also regenerates the very nature and life of God in us so that we become like Him. We become sons of the living God so we can call him Abba Father, for we did not receive a spirit of slavery but the Spirit of sonship, by whom we cry, "Abba! Father!" (Romans 8:15). For it is written "Love has been perfected among us in this: that we may have boldness in the day of judgment; because **AS HE IS, SO ARE WE IN THIS WORLD**" (1 John 4:17).

RESTORATION

Being purchased by the blood and regenerated by the blood we are restored into our heavenly position. We are brought near to God who sacked Adam (man) from His presence because of sin.

> *For it is written "But now in Christ Jesus you who once were far off have been brought near by the blood of Christ. For He Himself is our peace, who*

has made both one, and has broken down the middle wall of separation"

—*Ephesians 2:13-14*

When God had satisfied himself and fulfilled the requirement of shedding of Jesus, the scriptures point out that Jesus cried out with a loud voice, and yielded up His spirit, then, the veil of the temple was torn in two from top to bottom; and the earth quaked, and the rocks were split … (Matthew 27:50-51). Every limitation to us getting to near God was broken. The way was paved for us to easily reach our Heavenly Father, thus our restoration into the Heavenly Family. Scriptures therefore declare that we are no longer strangers and foreigners, but fellow citizens with the saints and members of the household of God (Ephesians 2:19). We are raised together with Jesus Christ and seated with him in high places as joint-heirs (Ephesians 2:6; Romans 8:17). Our relationship, inheritance, position and place in God is restored.

WHY THE BLOOD IN PRAYER?

W e have been enlightened in the previous pages that the blood of Jesus is the value offered to meet the justice requirement of God for our salvation. It is the blood that gives God the right to carry out His wish for man, meet our various needs and act in our favour without being unjust (Read Rom.3:23-26).

The blood has become evidence (proof) that nullifies the holdings and accusations of Satan against the believer. All accusations of Satan against you have been taken care of by the blood of Jesus. Employing the blood in prayer is like a presentation of an undeniable evidence in the court of law that shuts up the accuser and nullifies his claims. It is the receipt that justifies you in the prayer room (law court).

Glory be to God, the blood, apart from being the price for the emancipation of man from the dominion of Satan, also serves us a receipt (a proof) that reminds Satan of his defeat. It tells Satan that he has no business in your life. Satan doesn't want to hear this because it overrules his actions and claims. Reference to the blood of Jesus in prayer makes Satan powerless and useless. This is the reason why you must employ the blood in your prayer.

The blood of Jesus is the blood of the new covenant (Heb.10:29). It is the seal of New Testament. That is to say that making reference to the blood of Jesus in prayer, reminds God of the covenant He has with us. It is like saying "Daddy remember the deal". The engagement of the blood in prayer tends to bind God through His integrity to act in our favour. Involving the blood in prayer means that your deeds are not the grounds upon which God should answer you but upon the grounds of the blood of Jesus that was shed on the cross. In other words, the blood invokes the mercy of God for you.

In the light of these unsearchable efficacy of the blood of Jesus in prayer, the next pages provide precepts on praying with the blood. Practicing and developing the habit of engaging the blood in prayer will add a great potency to your prayer. Remember, they overcame the devil by the blood of the lamp and the word their testimony. Put the devil to where he belongs through the blood of our Lord Jesus Christ.

Prayer Quotes by A-A Freddy

1. "Show me a man of genuine humility and I will show you a man of fervent prayer"

2. "Humble men pray and prayer humbles men"

33 DAYS OF PRAYER

DAY 1

And according to the law almost all things are purified with blood, and without shedding of blood there is no remission of sins.

—*Hebrews 9:22 (NKJV)*

I thank you oh Lord God for the shedding of the precious blood of my savior Jesus Christ to eternally forgive my sins. For without the shedding of the blood of Jesus Christ there would have been no eternal remission for my sins. I was a wretched sinner but now a sanctified saint by the precious blood of Jesus Christ my savior. I thank you for making my life so precious in your sight to shed the very blood of your beloved son for the forgiveness of my sins. In Jesus name! Amen!

DAY 2

Therefore take heed to yourselves and to all the flock, among which the Holy Spirit has made you

overseers, to shepherd the church of God which HE PURCHASED WITH HIS OWN BLOOD.

—*Acts 20:28 (NKJV)*

Dear father I am very grateful for paying for my sins and for my life with the blood of Jesus Christ to give me a new life. By the power in the blood of Jesus I declare that my life has been fully paid for. Therefore, by this word I nullify any sales in the camp of the enemy against my life, health, marriage, business, finances and anything that concerns me. I declare that my Father in heaven paid fully for it all by the blood of Jesus Christ. Amen!

DAY 3

Therefore take heed to yourselves and to all the flock, among which the Holy Spirit has made you overseers, to shepherd the church of God which HE PURCHASED WITH HIS OWN BLOOD.

—*Acts 20:28 (NKJV)*

Father in heaven, I thank you for the blood of Jesus Christ. I stand on authority of your word in the book of Acts of the

Apostles 20:28 that you have bought me with your own blood and I declare to the devil that I am fully purchased by my Lord Jesus Christ and I belong to him. Therefore, now I take back my life, health, soul, body, marriage, finances from the camp of the enemy; witches, wizards, occults, demons, enchanters, diviners and I declare on authority of Yahweh's word that my life has been fully paid for, my health has been fully paid for, my soul has been fully paid for, my body has been fully paid for, my spirit has been fully paid for and regenerated, my destiny has been fully paid for. I declare no demon; witch or wizard can put me or anything associated with me on sale in their camps. Let the power in the blood of Jesus destroy and scatter every demonic and evil market transactions against my life, my prosperity and my destiny in the mighty name of Jesus Christ!!! Amen!

DAY 4

In Him we have redemption through His blood, the forgiveness of sins, according to the riches of His grace.

—*Ephesians 1:7 (NKJV)*

Dear Father in heaven I thank you for redeeming my life from the bondage of sin. Ephesians 1:7 makes me to understand that in you I have redemption. I thank you once again for this sweet redemption I have in you and I declare by the authority of this word that I am redeemed by the blood of Jesus Christ. Therefore, devil hear me, I belong to Jesus Christ and I belong to Yahweh!! I declare and decree that everything that concerns me is redeemed by the blood of Jesus Christ and I belong to him. My sins are forgiven according to the riches of God's grace. Therefore let every accusing hand fall and every accusing voice be silenced by the blood of my savior Jesus Christ!!! In Jesus mighty name!! Amen!

DAY 5

And from Jesus Christ, the faithful witness, the firstborn from the dead, and the ruler over the kings of the earth. To Him who loved us and washed us from our sins in His own blood

—Revelation 1:5 (NKJV)

Dear Father in heaven, thank you for setting me free from the bondage of sin by the blood of Jesus Christ my master and savior. Thank you for loving me and freeing me from my sins by your very blood. By the authority of this word I declare and enforce freedom from bondage of sin. I declare now that because my sins are washed and forgiven by the blood of Jesus Christ as I surrender my life to him. Devil, your strongholds and footholds in my life, business, finances and family is broken and destroyed now in Jesus mighty name!! I am loved by my Lord and Savior Jesus Christ!!!

DAY 6

Knowing that you were not redeemed with corruptible things, like silver or gold, from your aimless conduct received by tradition from your fathers, but with the precious blood of Christ, as of a lamb without blemish and without spot.

—*1 Peter 1:18-19 (NKJV)*

My father in heaven, thank you over and over again for freedom from sin and freedom from captivity of sin I have received through the shedding of the precious, holy blood of Jesus Christ. I declare and decree by authority of this word that by my redemption through the blood of Jesus Christ, I am free from sickness and diseases resulting from sin, I am free from poverty resulting from sin, I am free from curse resulting from sin, I am free from disgrace resulting from sin, I am free from debt resulting from sin, I am free from death resulting from sin, I am free from aimless conduct handed down to me by tradition from my fathers, I am free from the power of sin and death. Thank you, Father for the value you have placed on my life in Jesus mighty name!! Amen!!

DAY 7

That at that time you were without Christ, being aliens from the commonwealth of Israel and strangers from the covenants of promise, having no hope and without God in the world. But now in Christ Jesus you who once were far off have been brought near by the blood of Christ.
—*Ephesians 2:12-13 (NKJV)*

Dear Lord, I thank you for bringing me near to you and into your Kingdom by the blood of Jesus Christ. I was an enemy but now your child and your friend. Thank you Lord, for this privilege to be near to you and hidden from darkness, sin and the devil because in you there is light and no darkness at all. I pray in Jesus name! Amen!

DAY 8

For the LORD will pass through to strike the Egyptians; and when He sees the blood on the lintel and on the two doorposts, the LORD will pass over the door and not allow the destroyer to come into your houses to strike you.

—Exodus 12:23 (NKJV)

In the name of Jesus Christ my Savior and King, I take divine insurance by the Blood of Jesus Christ against spiritual and physical accidents, disasters and tragedy that the enemy has projected against my family this month. I declare that my household is secured and protected, Amen!

DAY 9

'...It is the Passover sacrifice of the LORD, who passed over the houses of the children of Israel in Egypt when He struck the Egyptians and delivered our households.'

—*Exodus 12:27 (NKJV)*

In the name of Jesus, I plead the Blood of Jesus over all access points in my household be it the vehicle, motorcycle, TV, radio, mobile phones, gifts and other items purchased. By the precious blood of Jesus, I cancel and dismantle every demonic plans assigned against any access points in my home, Amen!

DAY 10

And they shall take some of the blood and put it on the two doorposts and on the lintel of the houses where they eat it.

—*Exodus 12:7 (NKJV)*

Father, in heaven, just as you commanded Moses to tell the Israelites to take the blood of the lamb and put it on the sides and tops of the door-frames of their houses. Therefore, by this same spiritual obedience, I plead the Blood of Jesus over the doorways and windows of my home and against any demonic entity in human or animal form that enter my home and anything belonging to me. In the name of Jesus Christ, I render their plans and strategies useless and destroyed by the blood of Jesus Christ!! Amen!

DAY 11

To Jesus the Mediator of the new covenant and to the blood of sprinkling that speaks better things than that of Abel.

—*Hebrews 12:24 (NKJV)*

Father, I thank you for the benefits and provisions of the blood of Jesus available to my family. Today, I stand on the ground of the blood of Jesus to proclaim my family's freedom and victory over sin, Satan and his agents. I employ the blood to perpetually speak in my family in the name of Jesus Christ, Amen!

DAY 12

Knowing that you were not redeemed with corruptible things, like silver and gold, from your aimless conduct received by tradition from your fathers, but with the precious blood of Christ, as of a lamb without blemish and without spot.

—*1 Peter 1:18-19 (NKJV)*

Father, I thank you for redeeming my life with the precious blood of Christ and not with corruptible things. Today, I walk in this consciousness knowing that I am living a victorious life in Christ through the blood, Amen!

DAY 13

Let us therefore come boldly to the throne of grace, that we may obtain mercy and find grace to help in time of need.

—*Hebrews 4:16 (NKJV)*

Therefore, by honoring this invitation, I do not come on my own accord rather, through the Blood of Jesus. I come knowing that I am justified, sanctified and made holy with God's holiness and I have access to my Heavenly Father's throne without fear, intimidation or inferiority complex, Amen!

DAY 14

Much more then, having now been justified by His blood, we shall be saved from wrath through Him.

—Romans 5:9 (NKJV)

Father in heaven, by this word I have been justified by the blood of Jesus Christ. Therefore I thank you for my justification. I was once condemned and deserved to be punished for my sins but the blood of Jesus has justified me. Glory to your name oh Father in Jesus mighty name!! Amen!!

DAY 15

Being justified freely by His grace through the redemption that is in Christ Jesus, whom God set forth as propitiation by His blood, through faith, to demonstrate His righteousness, because in His forbearance God had passed over the sins that were previously committed.

—Romans 3:24-25 (NKJV)

Dear Lord I adore you for my justification through redemption that came to me through the shedding of the blood of Jesus Christ my Lord as I believed according to Romans 3:24-25. By this word I declared now that I am freely justified. Therefore no demonic and witchcraft accusations against me shall stand. Let every platform and grounds for demonic and witchcraft accusations against my life, family, finances, Joy, peace, and career catch fire now and be utterly destroyed now in the mighty name of Jesus Christ!!! Amen!!

DAY 16

No weapon formed against you shall prosper, And every tongue which rises against you in judgment You shall condemn. This is the heritage of the servants of the LORD, And their righteousness is from Me," Says the LORD.

—*Isaiah 54:17 (NKJV)*

I stand this day on the authority of the word of God which is truth and absolute truth and declare by faith that by the shedding of the blood of Jesus Christ I am freely justified, therefore, no weapon fashioned against me shall prosper. I take hold of my heritage through the blood of Jesus Christ and I condemn every tongue that rises against me and my household in judgment in the name of Jesus Christ, Amen!!

DAY 17

There is therefore now no condemnation to those who are in Christ Jesus, who do not walk according to the flesh, but according to the Spirit.
—*Romans 8:1 (NKJV)*

I declare this day that because I am justified by the blood of Jesus Christ, I walk in divine justification. I confess and enforce the word of the Lord my God that there is therefore now no condemnation for me. Let every demonic accusing hand and finger pointing at me scatter by the power in the blood of Jesus Christ, Amen!!

DAY 18

The hope of the righteous will be gladness, But the expectation of the wicked will perish.

—*Proverbs 10:28 (NKJV)*

By the blood of my justification, the precious blood of Jesus Christ, let every blood thirsty demons operating in my household be utterly destroyed!! Let the voice of evil blood of my forefathers and ancestors crying out for vengeance against my generation be silence by the voice of blood of Jesus Christ that speaks my justification!!! I declare and decree now that by virtue of the shed blood of my Lord Jesus Christ the desire of the wicked against my life, family, career and destiny are cut short in the mighty name of Jesus Christ!!

DAY 19

Not with the blood of goats and calves, but with His own blood He entered the Most Holy Place once for all, having obtained eternal redemption.

—*Hebrews 9:12 (NKJV)*

Father, in heaven, I thank you for my justification through the blood of Jesus Christ. I stand in the authority of your word and I declare that by the blood of Jesus Christ my Lord which he presented in the most holy place once and for all, for my redemption and to justify me freely, let every accusations and condemnation against my life and destiny that is responsible for delay of my miracles, failure at the edge of success, stagnation, fruitless efforts, delayed and denied promotion, satanic prophecies and evil diversions be destroyed now by the power in the blood of Jesus Christ, in the name of Jesus Christ! Amen!

DAY 20

Not with the blood of goats and calves, but with His own blood He entered the Most Holy Place once for all, having obtained eternal redemption.
—Hebrews 9:12 (NKJV)

My lovely father in heaven I give you glory and worship you for my redemption through the precious sinless blood of my Lord Jesus Christ. Right now I declare that my life is precious in the sight of my father who has placed my life higher than the blood of goats and calves and all other animals and humans. Therefore, no blood sacrifices against my life shall stand. I have been purchased and redeemed by the sinless, spotless, most powerful and highest blood every shed on this earth. Thank you Father in the name of Jesus Christ!!!! Amen!!!!

DAY 21

Therefore Jesus also, that He might sanctify the people with His own blood, suffered outside the gate.

—*Hebrews 13:12 (NKJV)*

Dear father in heaven, Jesus Christ my Lord suffered outside the city gate to make me holy through his own blood, Oh Lord my God I owe my life to you and I owe you thanks for laying down your life to make me Holy who was once a sinner. I thank you for making me Holy. I confess on the authority of the word that I am holy, my thoughts are holy, my heart desires are holy, and my life is holy. Jesus Christ has made me holy. I cannot be corrupted by this world because I am born again not of corruptible seed but incorruptible seed according to 1 Peter 1:23. In Jesus name! Amen!

DAY 22

Having wiped out the handwriting of requirements that was against us, which was

contrary to us. And He has taken it out of the way,
having nailed it to the cross.

—*Colossians 2:14 (NKJV)*

Father in heaven, I thank you for your wonderful word in Colossians 2:14. By this word I stand in authority and I command every evil ordinances enacted by ancestors, family, friends, evil agreements, exchanges, vows or transactions working against my life, family, finances, marriage, career and destiny to be canceled and crushed by the power in the blood of Jesus Christ!! I declare that any demonic requirements whether lawful or unlawful that was against me and my family is broken by the power in the blood of Jesus Christ! In the name of Jesus Christ! Amen!

DAY 23

I have been crucified with Christ; it is no longer I
who live, but Christ lives in me; and the life which
I now live in the flesh I live by faith in the Son of
God, who loved me and gave Himself for me.

—*Galatians 2:20 (NKJV)*

Lord, I thank you for the provision of the blood of Jesus, if not for this precious blood, where would I have been. Father, let the blood of Christ speak continually for me this week even in places I cannot speak for myself, Amen!

DAY 24

That at that time you were without Christ, being aliens from the commonwealth of Israel and strangers from the covenants of promise, having no hope and without God in the world. But now in Christ Jesus you who once were far off have been brought near by the blood of Christ.

—Ephesians 2:12-13 (NKJV)

Everlasting Father, I am eternally grateful for the blood of my Lord Jesus Christ. I thank you that because of the shed blood, I who was at one time separated from Christ, alienated from the commonwealth of Israel, and a stranger to the covenants of your promise, without hope in this world have now been brought near to you by the shed blood of Jesus

Christ. I thank you dear father and I praise your holy name in Jesus mighty name, Amen!!

DAY 25

That at that time you were without Christ, being aliens from the commonwealth of Israel and strangers from the covenants of promise, having no hope and without God in the world. But now in Christ Jesus you who once were far off have been brought near by the blood of Christ.

—*Ephesians 2:12-13 (NKJV)*

Dear father, I worship your Holy name for the salvation you have given me through the shed blood of my Lord Jesus Christ. I stand on the authority of your word in Ephesians 2:12-13 and I declare that I am a member of the body of Christ, I am a member of the commonwealth of Israel, I am a partaker of the your covenants of promise, and Christ in me is the hope of glory for my life. Therefore, from this day I take hold of every blessing due me as a member of the commonwealth of Israel and a partaker of covenants of promise of my father in heaven in Jesus mighty name! Amen!

DAY 26

For the life of the flesh is in the blood.
            —*Leviticus 17:11a (NKJV)*

Dear father, thank you for the blood of Jesus Christ. On this day I stand upon the authority of your word and I declare that because I am a member of the heavenly family and I have the life of Christ, the blood of Jesus Christ flows within me according to Leviticus 17:11. I declare that I carry the DNA of my heavenly father in the name of Jesus Christ!! Amen!!

DAY 27

Knowing that you were not redeemed with corruptible things, like silver and gold, from your aimless conduct received by tradition from your fathers, but with the precious blood of Christ, as of a lamb without blemish and without spot.

—*1 Peter 1:18-19 (NKJV)*

Dear Lord, I confess that I have been redeemed from the empty way of life handed down to me from my ancestors. I thank you father for my redemption and I declare by authority of this word that let every empty way of life handed over to me by my ancestors be destroyed by the power in the precious blood of Jesus! Amen!!

DAY 28

Likewise He also took the cup after supper, saying, "This cup is the new covenant in My blood, which is shed for you.

—*Luke 22:20 (NKJV)*

Father in heaven I thank you for the shed blood of Jesus Christ. I thank you for the new covenant I have in Christ Jesus because of his blood which he poured out for me. I declare that by virtue of the Word of God that evil covenants fighting against my destiny, children, marriage, career, finances are broken now by the power in the blood of Jesus Christ! Amen!

DAY 29

To Jesus the Mediator of the new covenant and to the blood of sprinkling that speaks better things than that of Abel.

—*Hebrews 12:24 (NKJV)*

Father in heaven, I thank you for this word. Right now I stand on the authority of this word and I ask for the sprinkling of the blood of Jesus Christ over my life and family. Let the voice of the blood of Jesus be activated in my life. Let the better things spoken by the blood of Jesus Christ in my life manifest now in the mighty name of Jesus Christ, Amen!!

DAY 30

Oh, give thanks to the LORD, for He is good! For His mercy endures forever. Let the redeemed of the LORD say so, Whom He has redeemed from the hand of the enemy,

—Psalm 107:1-2 (NKJV)

Dear Father, I give you thanks for you are good and love endures forever. I thank you for my redemption through the shed blood of my Lord Jesus Christ. According to your word in Psalm 107:2; Let the redeemed of the Lord tell their story— those you redeemed from the hand of the foe. I bless your Holy name dear Father, Yahweh. Thank you for redemption from the hands of the enemy and his wickedness. Hallelujah I will declare your goodness and love to the nations and to generations. Thank you for redemption from the wicked plans and agenda of the enemy for my life. Your name is glorious oh Lord. I worship you In the name of Jesus Christ!! Amen!!

DAY 31

> *How much more shall the blood of Christ, who through the eternal Spirit offered Himself without spot to God, cleanse your conscience from dead works to serve the living God?*
>
> *—Hebrews 9:14 (NKJV)*

My Father in heaven, I thank you for the blood of Jesus Christ that cleanses my sins and make me pure and whole in your sight. I ask for the continual cleansing of the blood of Jesus Christ in my life. I confess sins of omissions and commissions and any disobedience on my side. I ask this day that the blood of Christ, who through the eternal Spirit offered himself unblemished to you cleanses my conscience from acts that lead to death, so that I may serve you well oh Daddy. In Jesus mighty name!! Amen!

DAY 32

> *Now may the God of peace who brought up our Lord Jesus from the dead, that great Shepherd of*

the sheep, through the blood of the everlasting covenant, make you complete in every good work to do His will, working in you what is well pleasing in His sight, through Jesus Christ, to whom be glory forever and ever. Amen

—*Hebrews 13:20-21 (NKJV)*

Dear Father in heaven, I thank you for this day and again for the blood of Jesus Christ shed for me; the blood of a new and eternal covenant you have for me. Dear Lord I pray this day that by this new covenant equip me with every good thing for doing your will, and Lord my God work in me this day to do what is pleasing to you, through Jesus Christ, to Him be glory for ever and ever. Amen.

DAY 33

And they sang a new song, saying: "You are worthy to take the scroll, And to open its seals; For You were slain, And have redeemed us to God by Your blood Out of every tribe and tongue and people and nation, And have made us kings and

priests to our God; And we shall reign on the earth. "

—*Revelation 5:9-10 (NKJV)*

Father I thank you for this day. I will continually praise you for the innocent blood of Jesus Christ that was shed on the cross of Calvary for me. When I deserved to die, you spared me and crushed your only begotten son in my place. Father I thank you for the blood that purchased me from bondage and captivity into eternal freedom, from condemnation into justification, from slavery into a Kingdom, from worldliness into a holy priesthood. Oh Lord you are forever worthy of my praise and worship. I declare today according to your word in Rev 12:11 that I am an overcomer by blood of Jesus Christ!! In Jesus mighty name!! Amen!!

GFIOM

TOUCHING NATIONS WITH THE FINGER OF GOD

ABOUT THE BOOK

In this book, the reader is enlightened about the value God placed on man to shed the blood of Jesus Christ to meet the justice requirement for man's salvation. The reader is encouraged to employ the blood of Jesus in prayer which is an undeniable evidence that shuts up the accuser of the brethren and nullifies his claims in a believer's life. The book demonstrates and teaches the use of the blood of Jesus Christ; the blood of the new covenant, for Christians by providing precepts and engaging the reader on praying for 33 days with reference to the blood of Jesus, the Christ. Practicing and developing the habit of engaging and referring to the blood in prayer will add great potency to the prayers of the reader.

ABOUT THE AUTHOR

Frederick Amon-Armah is the president and founder of God's Finger International Outreach Ministry. He has a strong passion to preach the Gospel of the Lord Jesus Christ to the lost in the nations of the world. He is an evangelist, preacher and teacher of the Gospel, a revivalist, and a church planter by calling. He is an Agricultural Economist by profession. He holds a Bachelor's Degree in Agricultural Economics from the University of Ghana and a Master's Degree in same field from Dalhousie University in Canada. He is currently a Bible Student at the Assemblies of God Theological Seminary, Northern Campus, Ghana. He is married to a beautiful wife, Diana Amon-Armah and blessed with three lovely children.

www.ingramcontent.com/pod-product-compliance
Lightning Source LLC
Chambersburg PA
CBHW071732020426
42331CB00008B/2002